*I Had a MGB [...] del in 1969 — It nee[...] — on 5th Gear [...] I had [...] 955.) apart from bad leg cramps it was OK!*

*98[...]*
*2018*

# Handbook for the

# M G B

**ROADSTER**
**GT COUPÉ**
**from 1962**

------------------------------------------------

## PIET OLYSLAGER MSIA MSAE

## NELSON

THOMAS NELSON AND SONS LTD
36 Park Street London W1
P.O. Box 336 Apapa Lagos
P.O. Box 25012 Nairobi
P.O. Box No. 21149 Dar es Salaam
77 Coffee Street San Fernando Trinidad
THOMAS NELSON (AUSTRALIA) LTD
597 Little Collins Street Melbourne C1
THOMAS NELSON AND SONS (CANADA) LTD
81 Curlew Drive Don Mills Ontario
THOMAS NELSON AND SONS (SOUTH AFRICA) (PTY) LTD
P.O. Box 9881 Johannesburg
THOMAS NELSON AND SONS
Copewood and Davis Streets Camden 3, N.J.

English language edition

Printed in Great Britain by GALLEON PRINTERS LIMITED, HAZEL GROVE, CHESHIRE.

iv

# Contents

## SPECIAL NOTE

*Although every care is taken to ensure accuracy and completeness in compiling this book, no liability can be accepted for damage, loss or injury caused by any errors or omissions in the information given.*

# Preface

THIS MANUAL is intended to supplement (not to replace) the instruction book issued with the car by the manufacturer. It contains more detailed information on the maintenance and repair of the MGB without being, or pretending to be, a fully comprehensive workshop manual.

The early sections of the book contain general information essential for both owner-driver and mechanic. They give full details about the models covered so that the reader does not have to refer to many different publications in order to find correct model designations, serial numbers, major modifications, prices, dimensions, lubrication, maintenance and other information.

The section *Repair Data* has been compiled and presented on the assumption that the reader knows something about repair work. Elementary procedures have therefore been omitted and the space has been devoted to more advanced information. Readers who are not qualified to carry out repairs and adjustments are strongly advised to leave them to official BMC dealers or distributors, whose mechanics possess special equipment and are fully informed about the latest modifications and design changes. Often it will be more economical to replace a component by either a new or a factory-reconditioned unit rather than attempt to repair it. In all cases of doubt it will pay to consult a dealer.

All the important dimensions, tolerances and other specifications are presented in convenient tabular form at the end of the book, followed by an engine fault-finding chart.

PIET OLYSLAGER, MSAE, MSAI

Fig. 1. MGB Roadster with wire spoke wheels

Fig. 2. MGB Roadster with disc wheels

# General

## INTRODUCTION

The M.G. Series MGB Roadster was introduced by the M.G. Car Company Ltd., Abingdon-on-Thames, Berkshire, on 20th September, 1962, and made its public debut at the Earls Court Motor Show in London during the following month.

MGB production, which actually commenced in July 1962, has now exceeded the 75,000 figure and the only major modification so far has been the introduction of a five-bearing crankshaft for its 1798 cc BMC 'B' Series engine.

However, an additional model was introduced on 19th October 1965 in the form of a closed coupé version, known as the MGB GT.

The MGB, which broke with established M.G. practice by having wind-up windows and an integrally constructed body-cum-chassis shell, was designed as a successor to the MGA to carry on the modern tradition of sports cars. Of the MGA series (1500, Twin Cam, 1600 and 1600 Mk II), well over 100,000 had been produced from 1955 when it succeeded the Midget 'T'-types. The MGA was the first revolutionary departure from the old traditional and familiar M.G. body shape and brought an end to the Spartan line with square radiator and slab tank, which had been in vogue for 23 years, from the 1932 'J2' to the 'TF' of 1953–55.

The M.G. Car Company belongs to Morris Motors Limited, founded by the late Lord Nuffield and now part of the British Motor Corporation, and its history goes back to 1922, when Cecil Kimber became manager of the Morris Garages, in Oxford, from which the first Morris cars had emanated. Kimber began building deluxe, semi-sporting versions of the contemporary Morris touring cars and by March 1924 these had become known as the M.G. Special Sports models (M.G. = Morris Garages). In 1925 Kimber won a gold medal in the Lands End Trial with his first two-seater sports M.G. of original design, and this car he always referred to as 'Old Number One'—the beginning of the truly sporting M.G. tradition—although the M.G. Car Co. Ltd. was not founded as a separate marque until production moved to Abingdon in 1929. The first model built there was the first of a long line of M.G. Midgets—the 'M'-type with an 847 cc ohc engine. The name 'Midget' was not used for the 1955 MGA, but was revived in June 1961 with the introduction of the new 948 cc Midget Mark I, which in 1966 developed into the current 1275 cc Mark III and which is basically similar to BMC's Austin-Healey Sprite two-seater sports car.

It is interesting to note that there has been a 'B'-type M.G. before: the 1930 M.G. 2½-litre Six Mk III—'Tigress'. Only five of these cars were produced, including an experimental one, and two of them still exist. The 'Tigress' was the first M.G. to be built specifically for racing.

Since their inception, M.G. have collected an impressive number of records, trophies and awards. These date from 1930 and culminated in 1959 with the land speed record for a 1½-litre car in excess of 250 mph. It was achieved with an experimental model, EX181, powered by a supercharged MGA Twin Cam engine and driven by Phil Hill.

Fig. 3. MGB GT Coupe, threequarter front view

Fig. 4. MGB GT Coupe, threequarter rear view

## DESCRIPTION

The MGB is an open, two-door, two-seater sports roadster (with occasional rear seating) of all-steel integral ('monocoque') construction. The MGB GT is basically the same car but has a more spacious closed coupé body with 'fast-back' styling.

The engine is a variation of the BMC four-cylinder ohv (pushrod) 'B' Series power unit, in this form having a cubic capacity of 1798 cc and developing 94 bhp at 5500 rpm. In 1964 this engine was modified to have a five-bearing crankshaft and, working with $8 \cdot 8 : 1$ compression ratio, it now develops 95 bhp at 5400 rpm. Twin SU semi-downdraught carburettors are fitted, each provided with an air-cleaner.

A Borg and Beck single dry plate clutch with diaphragm spring and hydraulic actuation transmits the engine power to the four-speed gearbox with remote control and synchromesh on second, third and top gear. Overdrive (Laycock de Normanville) on third and top gear is among the MGB's optional extras. The three-quarter floating rear axle with hypoid bevel final drive has a gear ratio of $3 \cdot 909 : 1$.

Lockheed hydraulic braking is used, employing discs at the front and drums at the rear.

Suspension is conventional: independent with coil springs at front, semi-elliptic leaf springs at rear. The GT coupé has an anti-roll bar as standard fitting and stronger front and rear springs. An anti-roll bar is also available as an optional extra on the roadster.

The steering gear is of the rack-and-pinion type with spring-spoke steering wheel.

4J x 14 well-base disc-type wheels (5J on GT) fitted with 5.60–14 tubed nylon tyres are standard equipment; $4\frac{1}{2}$J x 14 wire spoke wheels and/or 155–14 (165–14 on GT) radial-ply tyres are optional equipment.

Export specification includes oil cooler (standard on all five-bearing crankshaft engines), front and rear bumper over-riders, mph or kph speedometer, headlighting according to market and twin horns. For certain export territories a lower compression ratio is also available.

A fibreglass hardtop became available as a BMC optional extra for the roadster in June 1963.

## IDENTIFICATION

**Engine number:**

The engine number is stamped on a plate secured to the right-hand side of the cylinder block. The actual engine serial number is prefixed by various letters and numbers representing, in code, the power unit specification. The prefix is divided into three groups, indicating the engine capacity and model, gearbox and ancillary equipment, and compression ratio.

Example of engine number: 18 GB–RU–H–46159, in which

| | | |
|---|---|---|
| 18GB | = | MGB 1800 five-bearing crankshaft engine with closed-circuit breathing (18G=three-bearing engine with conventional crankcase ventilation; 18GA=three-bearing engine with closed-circuit breathing). |
| R | = | Laycock de Normanville overdrive (optional extra). |
| U | = | Central gear-change gearbox. |
| H | = | High-compression ratio ($8 \cdot 8 : 1$; L=low-compression ration, $8 \cdot 0 : 1$). |
| 46159 | = | actual engine serial number. |

**Car (or chassis) number:**
The car number is stamped on a plate secured to the top left-hand side of the front bulkhead.

NOTE: On some cars for the USA this number is stamped on a plate fixed to the inside of the front right-hand 'chassis' member, below the front suspension cross-member.

The actual serial number is prefixed by the car model series designation, as follows:
GHN3 – MGB Roadster
GHD3 – MGB GT Coupé
Suffix 'L' denotes left-hand drive.

**Car serial numbers** (approximate and for guidance only):

| | |
|---|---|
| July 1962 (starting) | 101 |
| January 1963 | 4550 |
| January 1964 | 27280 |
| January 1965 | 53640 |
| January 1966 | 75250 |

**Gearbox number:**
The gearbox number is stamped on the top of the gearbox, adjacent to the oil-level dipstick.

**Rear axle number:**
This number is stamped on the front of the axle tube on the left-hand side, adjacent to the spring seat.

## MODIFICATIONS

NOTE: For modifications of a purely technical nature see under *Repair Data*.

**1963:**
In January the Laycock de Normanville overdrive operating on third and top gear was introduced as an optional extra.

In February, at car number 6693, a redesigned parking brake lever was introduced and during May, at car number 11313, the rear leaf springs were modified.

**1964:**
In September the engine crankcase ventilation system was modified and now is of the 'closed circuit' type, incorporating an oil separator which removes unburnt oil from the crankcase fumes (car No. 31021; addition of letter B to engine number prefix). The following modifications and improvements were announced at the London Motor Show in October and commenced from car No. 48766: five-bearing crankshaft (introduced with the BMC 1800 ADO. 17), oil-cooler as standard equipment on all cars (previously only on export models, optional extra for home market), electrically-operated rev-counter (replacing mechanical type), and new thermal-type fuel gauge.

**1965:**
In March the capacity of the fuel tank was increased from 10 to 12 Imp gallons (12 to 14·4 US gallons), as from car No. 56743, and in June (car No. 64313) modified propeller shaft universal joints were introduced featuring sealed bearings requiring no periodical greasing.

**1966:**
Positions of lighting switch and windscreen-washer control on dash were interchanged for easier operation. Headlight flasher switch now standard.

Fig. 5. MGB Coupe designed by Coune, a Belgian stylist, and introduced at the
Amsterdam Motor Show in February 1965

Fig. 6. MGB with optional hard top

Fig. 7. MGB GT left-hand drive, showing access to rear compartment

Fig. 8. MGB, front compartment and facia

Fig. 9. MGB GT, front compartment and facia

## PRICES

UK prices are home retail ex-works prices.

|  | Basic | P.T. | Total |
|---|---|---|---|
| September 1962, MGB: | £690.0.0 | £259.15.3 | £949.15.3 |
| November 1962, MGB: | £690.0.0 | £144.6.3 | £834.6.3 |
| October 1963, MGB: | £690.0.0 | £144.6.3 | £834.6.3 |
| October 1964, MGB: | £690.0.0 | £144.6.3 | £834.6.3 |
| November 1965, MGB: | £706.10.0 | £148.15.0 | £855.5.0 |
| MGB GT: | £825.0.0 | £173.8.9 | £998.8.9 |
| June 1966, MGB: | £706.10.0 | £148.15.0 | £855.5.0 |
| MGB GT: | £825.0.0 | £173.8.9 | £998.8.9 |
| January 1967, MGB: | £706.10.0 | £163.10.0 | £870.0.0 |
| MGB GT: | £825.0.0 | £190.15.0 | £1015.15.0 |

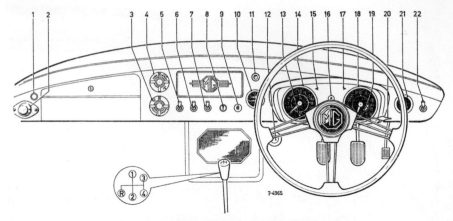

Fig. 10. Instruments and controls (right-hand drive shown)

**Optional extras (1965-66), including P.T.:**

| Overdrive: | £60.8.4 | Tonneau cover*: | £9.13.4 |
| Hardtop*: | £72.10.0 | Anti-roll bar*: | £2.8.4 |
| Wire spoke wheels**: | £30.4.2 | White side-wall tyres**: | £7.11.1 |
| Heater: | £14.16.1 | SP41 tyres**: | £8.6.2 |
| Folding hood*: | £4.16.8 | Headlamp flasher*: | £1.4.2 |

\* Not applicable to MGB GT.  \*\* In lieu of standard equipment.

## INSTRUMENTS AND CONTROLS

1 Map-reading light switch
2 Map-reading light
3 Heater controls: air distribution
4 Heater controls: temperature regulation
5 Heater controls: blower switch
6 Windscreen-wiper switch
7 Light switch (1966 on: windscreen-washer control)
8 Ignition/starter switch
9 Choke control
10 Oil pressure and water temperature gauge
11 Windscreen-washer control (1966 on: light switch)
12 Dipper switch
13 Main beam warning light
14 Speedometer and mileage recorder
15 Direction-indicator warning light, left
16 Panel light switch
17 Direction-indicator warning light, right
18 Rev-counter
19 Dynamo/ignition warning light
20 Direction-indicator switch (and headlight flasher, when fitted)
21 Fuel gauge
22 Overdrive switch (when fitted)

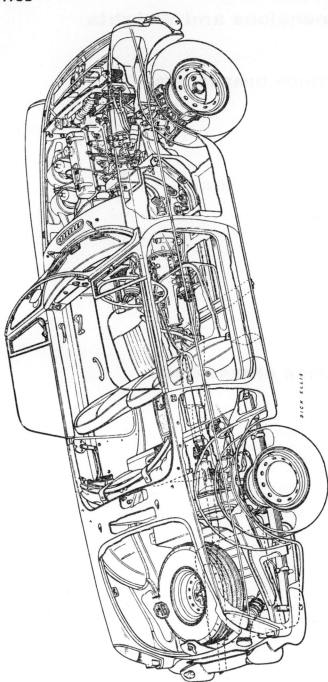

Fig. 11. MGB Roadster, ghost view

# Dimensions and Weights

## EXTERIOR DIMENSIONS

|  | *inches* | |
| --- | --- | --- |
|  | **MGB** | **MGB GT** |
| Wheelbase: | 91 | 91 |
| Track, front: | 49 | 49 |
| Track, rear: | 49¼ | 49¼ |
| Overall length (including overriders): | 153¼ | 153¼ |
| Overall width: | 60 | 60 |
| Overall height: | 49½ | 49¾ |
| Ground clearance: | 5 | 5 |
| Turning circle: | 32ft | 32ft |

## INTERIOR DIMENSIONS

| | MGB | MGB GT |
| --- | --- | --- |
| Pedals to front seat: | 17–24 | 17–24 |
| Steering wheel to seat: | 6 | 6 |
| Steering wheel to seat backrest: | 14½–21½ | 14½–21½ |
| Height over front seat: | 37 | 37 |
| Height of front seat: | 9 | 9 |
| Maximum adjustment of front seat: | 7½ | 7½ |
| Depth of front seat: | 19 | 19 |
| Front seat backrest to rear seat (maximum): | — | 6 |
| Height over rear seat: | — | 26 |
| Height of rear seat: | — | 13½ |
| Depth of rear seat: | — | 16 |
| Width of rear platform: | 16 | — |
| Width of front seats, each: | 18 | 18 |
| Width of rear seat: | 48½ | 47½ |
| Width between doors: | 50½ | 50½ |
| Shoulder width over front seats: | 46 | 46 |
| Maximum interior height: | 40 | 39 |
| Height of luggage compartment, maximum: | 16½ | 19½ |
| Width of luggage compartment: | 57 | 57 |
| Depth of luggage compartment: | 29½ | 29 |

### WEIGHTS

|                                                         | MGB      | MGB GT   |
|---------------------------------------------------------|----------|----------|
| Unladen weight:                                         | 1920 lb  | 2190 lb  |
| Kerbside weight (unladen, fuel tank half-full):         | 2030 lb  | 2310 lb  |
| Weight distribution (kerbside weight, front/rear):      | 53½/46½  | 50/50    |
| Maximum permissible gross weight:                       | 2430 lb  | 2660 lb  |

# Technical Specifications

### ENGINE

| | |
|---|---|
| Model: | 18G, 18GA* or 18GB** |
| Type: | four-stroke petrol, water-cooled |
| Number of cylinders: | four, in line |
| Valve arrangement: | overhead, pushrod-operated |
| Bore and stroke (in): | 3·16 x 3·5 |
| (mm): | 80·26 x 88·9 |
| Cubic capacity (cu in): | 109·6 |
| (cc): | 1798 |
| Compression ratio: | 8·8 or 8·0 : 1 |

|                                       | high compression | low compression |
|---------------------------------------|------------------|-----------------|
| Maximum bhp at rpm:                   | 95 at 5400***    | 91 at 5400      |
| Maximum bmep, lb/sq in at rpm:        | 152 at 3100      | 152 at 3100     |
| Maximum torque, lb ft at rpm:         | 110 at 3000***   | 105 at 3000     |
| Mean piston speed at max. bhp (ft/min): 3150 | | |
| Top gear mph at 1000 rpm: 17·9 (with overdrive, 22·3) | | |
| Carburettors: twin SU HS4 | | |

*Engine with closed-circuit crankcase ventilation.

**Engine with five-bearing crankshaft.

***Early models: 94 bhp at 5500 rpm, 107 lb ft at 3500 rpm

### TRANSMISSION

| | |
|---|---|
| Clutch: | single dry plate, 8 in |
| Gearbox: | four-speed, synchromesh on second, third, and top |
| Gearbox ratios (to 1): | 1·00, 1·37, 2·21, 3·64, R. 4·76 |
| Overdrive ratio (to 1): | 0·802 |
| Final drive and ratio (to 1): | hypoid bevel, 3·909 |
| Overall gear ratios (to 1): | 3·909 (o.d. 3·315), 5·3694 (o.d. 4·3062), 8·6557, 14·2143, R. 18·5881 |

## CHASSIS

| | |
|---|---|
| Chassis construction: | unitary, body-cum-chassis |
| Suspension, front: | independent, wishbones, coil springs (anti-roll bar standard on GT, optional on roadster) |
| Suspension, rear: | semi-elliptic leaf springs |
| Shock-absorbers | Armstrong hydraulic, lever type |
| Steering gear: | rack-and-pinion |
| Wheels and rim size, standard: | steel disc, 4J x 14 (5J on GT) |
| optional: | wire spoke, 4½J x 14 |
| Tyres, type and size, standard: | Dunlop Gold Seal C41, 5.60–14 (tubed) |
| optional: | Dunlop SP41 (tubed) 155–14 (165–14 on GT) |
| Brakes, type: | Lockheed; discs front, drums rear |
| Brakes, dimensions: | disc diameter 10¾in, drum diameter 10in rear linings 9 7/16 x 1¾in |

## ELECTRICAL EQUIPMENT

| | |
|---|---|
| Electrical system: | 12-volt |
| Battery: | twin 6-volt, 58 Ah |
| Earthing: | positive ($+$) |
| Ignition: | battery and coil |

## THEORETICAL ROAD SPEEDS

(Speeds in brackets apply when overdrive is engaged)

| | rpm | first gear (mph) | second gear (mph) | third gear (mph) | top gear (mph) | mean piston speed (ft/min) |
|---|---|---|---|---|---|---|
| (a) | 1000 | 4·9 | 8·1 | 13·1 (16·3) | 17·9 (22·3) | 583·3 |
| (b1) | 3000 | 14·7 | 24·3 | 39·3 (48·9) | 53·7 (66·9) | 1749·9 |
| (b2) | 3500 | 17·1 | 28·3 | 45·8 (57·0) | 62·6 (78·0) | 2041·5 |
| (c1) | 5400 | 26·5 | 43·7 | 70·7 (88·0) | 96·7 (120·4) | 3149·8 |
| (c2) | 5500 | 27·0 | 44·6 | 72·0 (89·6) | 98·4 (122·6) | 3208·2 |

(b)=rpm at maximum torque, later and early models respectively.
(c)=rpm at maximum bph, later and early models respectively.

## PERFORMANCE FIGURES

NOTE: These figures are approximate and should be considered to be fair averages. Figures in brackets are with overdrive engaged.

| | MGB | MGB GT |
|---|---|---|
| Maximum speed (mph), top gear: | 106 | 108 |
| third gear: | 78 (96) | 79 (98) |
| second gear: | 48 | 48 |
| first gear: | 28 | 29 |
| Acceleration times (sec.), 0–30 mph: | 4·6 | 4·0 |
| 0–14 mph: | 7·2 | 6·1 |
| 0–50 mph: | 9·0 | 8·7 |
| 0–60 mph: | 12·7 | 13·1 |
| 0–70 mph | 16·2 | 18·0 |
| 0–80 mph: | 21·2 | 23·9 |
| 0–90 mph: | 31·0 | 36·0 |
| standing quarter-mile: | 18·9 | 19·6 |

| (in top gear) | 20–40 mph: | 9·5 (14·9) | 11·0 (18·0) |
|---|---|---|---|
| | 30–50 mph: | 9·1 (14·9) | 9·8 (16·1) |
| | 40–60 mph: | 9·2 (14·8) | 10·6 (16·1) |
| | 50–70 mph: | 9·3 (14·4) | 12·3 (17·8) |
| | 60–80 mph: | 10·7 (16·2) | 14·5 (23·1) |
| | 70–90 mph: | 14·8 (26·9) | 20·0 (33·0) |
| Fuel consumption, touring (mpg): | | 30 | 30 |
| overall (mpg): | | 22 | 21 |
| Cruising range*: | | 260 | 250 |

*Based on 12-gallon fuel tank capacity of 1965–66 models.

# Lubrication and Maintenance

**Running-in speeds:**
During the first 500 miles do not exceed 45 mph in top gear and corresponding speeds in lower gears (2,500 rpm). Do not maintain this maximum speed for long periods. Avoid long periods of idling, full-throttle acceleration and over-revving of the engine. Never overload the engine; change down to a lower gear when necessary; the engine must be operated at normal rpm. After this initial period the speed may be progressively increased until the engine is fully run-in.

## GENERAL DATA

**Engine:**
Sump capacity, including filter:     7½ Imp pints (9 US pints)
Oil-cooler (when fitted):     ¾ Imp pint (0·9 US pint)
Oil viscosity:     tropical and temperate down to 5°C (41°F)—
SAE 40, SAE 20W/40, 20/50, 40/50
Extreme cold temperatures between 5°C (41°F) and —12°C (10°F)—SAE 20W, SAE 10W/30
Arctic conditions. Temperatures consistently below — 12° C (10° F) — SAE 10W, SAE, 5W/20

Oil dipstick: at right-hand side of engine.
Oil filler cap: on forward end of valve rocker cover.
Oil change interval: every 6000 miles. NOTE: If using monograde oil, every 3000 miles.
Oil drain plug: on right-hand side of sump.
Run the engine to warm-up the oil before draining the sump.
**Oil filter (renewable-element type):** Change engine oil filter element every 6000 miles with the engine oil change. The filter is located on the right-hand side of the engine and is released by undoing the central bolt securing the filter bowl to the filter head. Clean housing and renew filter element. Make sure that the sealing ring is correctly positioned, that all washers and seals are in their correct positions, and that the bowl is seated centrally on the seal.
**Air-cleaners (dry type):** Every 12,000 miles fit new air-cleaner elements. Unscrew bolts securing air-cleaners to the choke brackets and facing plates respectively, remove elements, clean casings and reassemble using new elements.
**Carburettors (SU):** Every 3000 miles top-up damper reservoirs with engine oil. Unscrew and withdraw the oil caps with their attached plungers and top-up with engine oil (SAE 20) to within ½ in above the tops of the hollow piston rods. Do not use a heavy-bodied lubricant.

**Ignition distributor:** Every 6000 miles remove rotor and apply a few drops of engine oil on screw thus exposed, one drop on breaker-arm pivot and a few drops on automatic advance mechanism through gap round cam spindle. Lightly smear cam profile with grease or oil.

**Dynamo:** Every 6000 miles add two drops of engine oil to the lubrication hole in the centre of the rear bearing plate. *Do not over-oil.*

Inspect and adjust dynamo driving belt but do not overtighten.

**Water pump:** Lubricate every 12,000 miles. Remove the plug from the housing and add a small quantity of grease.

**Gearbox and overdrive:**

Capacity: gearbox $4\frac{1}{2}$ Imp pints (5·6 US pints), gearbox and overdrive 5 Imp pints (6 US pints).

Oil viscosity: as for engine.

Oil level check: every 6000 miles check oil level with dipstick and replenish if necessary.

Combined filler plug and dipstick: located beneath rubber plug on the tunnel behind the speaker panel.

**Rear axle/Differential:**

Capacity: $2\frac{1}{4}$ Imp pints (2·7 US pints).

Oil grade: EP (Hypoid, extreme pressure) gear oil.

Oil viscosity: 32°C (90°F) down to —12°C (10°F): SAE 90 EP.

Oil-level check: every 6000 miles, replenish if necessary to the level of the filler plug.

**Steering gear:** Every 12,000 miles, lubricate steering rack with oil-gun (1 nipple, SAE 90 EP, 10 strokes maximum). Access to nipple is gained from above on right-hand drive cars and from below the radiator on left-hand drive cars (early roadsters only).

**Brake and clutch fluid reservoirs:** Every 3000 miles check the level of fluid in the reservoirs located on the engine bulkhead.

Fluid level should be maintained $\frac{1}{2}$ in (13 mm) below the bottom of the filler cap in each reservoir. Replenish with Lockheed Disc Brake Fluid (Series II). Do not use any substitute, as this may seriously affect the working of the system.

Visually inspect brake pipes for leakage and security. Rectify if necessary.

**Cooling system:** Capacity 10 Imp pints (12 US pints) including $\frac{1}{2}$ pint for heater.

Location of drain taps: left-hand side at bottom of the radiator and rear right-hand side of the cylinder block.

In frosty conditions it is necessary to protect the cooling system with an approved anti-freeze solution. When the outside temperature is between 0°C (32°F) and —18°C (0°F) use one part of anti-freeze to three parts of water.

NOTE: Never remove filler cap when engine is hot.

**Fuel tank:** Capacity 10 Imp gallons (12 US gallons); later models 12 Imp gallons (14·4 US gallons).

Fuel requirements (octane rating): compression ratio 8·8 to 1: above 98
compression ratio 8·0 to 1: above 93

**Grease nipples:** Every 3000 miles lubricate with grease-gun (lithium-based multi-purpose grease): the swivel pins (6 nipples), propeller shaft universal joints and sliding yoke (3 nipples), and parking brake cable (1 nipple). N.B. Later type propellor shaft universal joints have sealed bearings and do not require attention.

**Tyre pressures (lb/sq in; check when cold):**

| | Roadster | GT |
|---|---|---|
| *Standard tyres* (e.g. Dunlop Gold Seal C41): | | |
| Normal conditions, up to 90mph, front/rear: | 18/18 | 20/24 |

| | | |
|---|---|---|
| Sustained speeds over 90 mph: | 24/24 | 26/30 |

*Radial-ply tyres* (e.g. Dunlop SP41):

| | | |
|---|---|---|
| Normal conditions, up to 90 mph, front/rear: | 21/24 | 21/24 |
| Sustained speeds over 90 mph: | 27/31 | 28/31 |

## ROUTINE MAINTENANCE

NOTE: See also *General Data* on page 15.
*Daily:* Check engine oil level, cooling system, fuel tank, tyres.
*Weekly:* Check battery electrolyte, tyre pressures.

### A. Every 3000 miles:

*A*1  Engine sump: drain (when hot) and refill. (Monograde oils only.)
*A*2  Swivel pins: lubricate with grease-gun (6 nipples).
*A*3  Propeller shaft front universal joint and sliding yoke: lubricate with grease-gun (1 or 2 nipples).
*A*4  Propeller shaft rear universal joint: lubricate with grease-gun (1 nipple, if fitted).
*A*5  Parking brake cable: lubricate with grease-gun (1 nipple).
*A*6  Carburettors: top-up dampers with engine oil; lubricate controls with engine oil.
*A*7  Brake and clutch fluid reservoirs: check fluid level; top-up if necessary.
Locks, hinges, key slots, safety catches, etc.: lubricate with a few drops of engine oil.
Door dovetails and striker plates: sparingly smear with grease.
Belt tension, spark plugs, automatic advance mechanism, battery fluid specific gravity, brake adjustment, brake linings and pipes, wheel nuts, tyres: check and if necessary clean and/or adjust.
Road wheels: interchange.

### B. Every 6000 miles:

*B*1  Engine sump: drain (when hot) and refill; clean oil-filter housing and renew element; check sealing washer.
*B*2  Gearbox and overdrive (if fitted): clean overdrive filter element; check oil level; top-up if necessary.
*B*3  Rear axle/Differential: check oil level; top-up if necessary.
*B*4  Ignition distributor: remove rotor and apply a few drops of engine oil on screw thus exposed, one drop on breaker-arm pivot and a few drops on automatic advance mechanism through gap round cam spindle. Lightly smear cam profile with grease or oil.
*B*5  Dynamo: lubricate rear bearing with a few drops of engine oil.
Valve clearances, contact breaker points, front wheel alignment, disc brake pads, rear spring anchorages and centre bolts, lights: check, and if necessary clean and/or adjust.

### C. Every 12,000 miles:

*C*1  Engine sump: after draining, flush out with flushing oil (early models only).
*C*2  Steering gear: lubricate with oil-gun (1 nipple, 10 strokes max., early roadsters only).
*C*3  Water pump: remove plug and sparingly lubricate with grease.
*C*4  Air-cleaner, dry type: replace paper elements.
Carburettors: dismantle and clean, lightly coat piston rods with engine oil.
Spark plugs: replace.

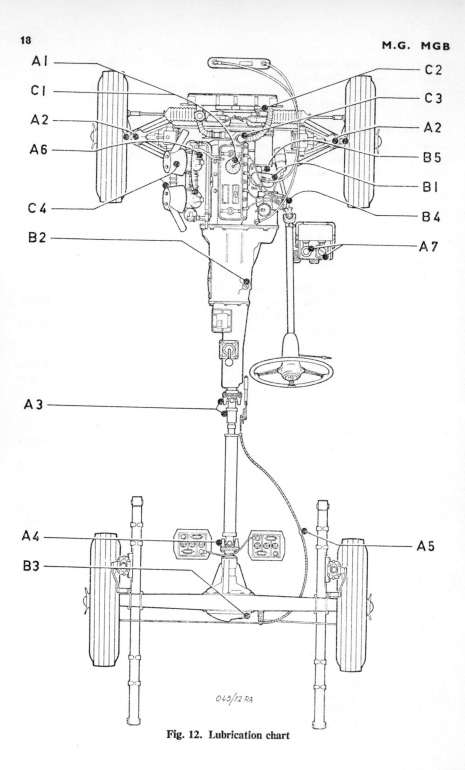

A 1
C 1
A 2
A 6
C 4
B 2
A 3
A 4
B 3

C 2
C 3
A 2
B 5
B 1
B 4
A 7
A 5

045/12 RA

**Fig. 12. Lubrication chart**

Crankcase closed breathing system (if fitted): clean breather valve, renew engine oil filler cap-cum-filter.

Steering mechanism and suspension: check for wear.

Cooling system: drain, flush out and refill.

Overdrive: drain gearbox, clean overdrive filter element, replace and refill.

# Repair Data

**Repairs are best performed by authorised BMC dealers, who possess special tools and the necessary experience. These data have been compiled from the official workshop manuals and other technical publications, supplied through the kind co-operation of The British Motor Corporation Ltd.**

## ENGINE

Description (Engine type 18G/18GA):

Water-cooled, four-cylinder, ohv petrol engine in line, built together with the single dry plate clutch and the all-sychronised four-speed gearbox.

The unit is mounted in the front of the vehicle on three flexible rubber mountings. The axial movement of the engine on its mounting rubbers is checked by means of a reaction or stabilizer rod fitted between the gearbox and the rear mounting crossmember.

The engine can be removed from the vehicle together with the gearbox or, alternatively, without the gearbox; if, however, the gearbox only needs servicing, the engine must be removed as well.

Engine cooling is obtained by means of a radiator, mounted transversely in front of the engine, a water pump of the impellor-type with a three- or, alternatively, a five-bladed fan, which is driven in tandem with the generator from the crankshaft pulley by means of a V-belt.

Quick engine warm-up and constant engine operating temperature are obtained by means of a bellows-type thermostat, which is situated in the thermostat housing, also forming the cooling water outlet pipe, on the front end of the cylinder head. The V-belt is adjusted in the conventional manner, by pivoting the generator away from or toward the engine as necessary. The cast-iron cylinder head, incorporating the overhead valve mechanism, is attached to the cast-iron cylinder block by means of studs and stud nuts. The valves are placed vertically and in line and are equipped with double valve springs; the valves are kept in place in the conventional BMC manner, employing a lower spring seating washer, a top-mounted spring retaining washer and two valve-keepers, which in turn are kept in place by means of retaining circlips. The valve stems are fitted with rubber O-ring type oil-seals to prevent oil from leaking into the combustion chambers. The valve seats are machined directly into the cylinder-head material. The valve guides are replaccable and are available in standard size only.

The forged steel valve rockers, provided with a drilling for the lubrication of the valve mechanism, are located on the hollow steel valve rockershaft; this shaft is attached to the cylinder head by means of four detachable rockershaft supports.

The separate inlet and exhaust manifolds are bolted to the left-hand side of the cylinder head; the manifolds are not joined to form a hot-spot and can be removed or installed separately.

The cast-iron cylinder block incorporates the upper half of the crankcase; no separate cylinder liners are used. If the cylinders, however, become worn beyond re-bore limits, new dry cylinder liners can be installed.

Fig. 13. Engine and gearbox, side view

The pistons are of the solid-skirt type and are fitted to the forged steel connecting rods of H-beam section by means of semi-floating piston pins, which are kept in place in the connecting-rod small ends by means of a pinch-bolt arrangement. Oversize pistons are available in several sizes (see *Technical Data*). Each piston is equipped with three compression rings, of which the lower two rings are tapered, and one oil control ring, all fitted above the piston pin.

The forged steel crankshaft runs in three main bearings, which consist of steel-backed half-bearing shell inserts, lined with copper/lead bearing material with indium overlay. The connecting-rod bearing steel-backed half-bearing shell inserts are lined with a similar bearing material. The main bearing shells, as well as the connecting-rod bearing shells, are available in standard and four undersizes. The crankshaft thrust and end-float are taken at the centre main bearing by means of four semi-circular thrust washers which are steel-backed and lined with bearing material, being seated in the machined half-grooves in the centre main bearing web and in the centre main-bearing cap. The main-bearing caps are secured by means of heavy studs and stud nuts.

The flywheel, with shrunk-on starter ring gear, is bolted onto the flange at the rear end of the crankshaft. The protruding front end of the crankshaft accommodates the double timing chain sprocket, a concave oil thrower ring and the crankshaft pulley; the sprocket and the crankshaft pulley are both fitted with a Woodruff key.

The camshaft runs in three replaceable bi-metal bearing bushes and is located in the left-hand side of the cylinder block; the camshaft end-float is taken by means of a bi-metal thrust flange which is fitted between the camshaft sprocket and the front camshaft bearing. The duplex timing chain is automatically tensioned by means of a Reynolds-type spring assisted hydraulic chain tensioner, the thrust block of which is forced against the chain by oil pressure.

The timing sprockets are aligned by adjustment shims placed behind the crankshaft sprocket. The camshaft operates the valve rockers indirectly by means of hollow steel valve tappets of the barrel type and steel pushrods.

The ignition distributor, which is equipped with vacuum and centrifugal advance mechanism, is located on the right-hand side of the engine and is driven by a helical gear, machined on the camshaft. The drive is transmitted by means of a separate drive spindle.

The rotor-type oil pump is located in the left-hand side of the cylinder block and is driven from the camshaft by means of a short drive shaft. The oil pump draws the oil via a wire gauze strainer out of the sump and forces it, via a drilling in the cylinder block, to a non-adjustable pressure relief valve, which is situated on the rear left-hand side of the cylinder block; from here the oil is fed to the main oil gallery through a cross-drilling in the cylinder block. The main oil gallery is a longitudinal drilling in the right-hand side of the cylinder block; part of the main oil gallery is formed by the mounting head of the externally mounted fullflow oil-filter with a replaceable micronic filter element. From the main oil gallery, the oil is fed through separate drillings to the crankshaft main bearings and from there via drillings in the crankshaft to the nearest connecting-rod bearings. The front, centre and rear camshaft bearings receive oil emerging from the front, centre and rear main bearing, respectively, through separate drillings in the cylinder block. From the camshaft bearings, oil is forced to the remaining components to be lubricated.

The timing-chain tensioner is pressure-fed and the timing gear is lubricated from the front camshaft bearing. Oil from the centre camshaft bearing supplies the oil-pump drive and the valve tappets with lubrication, whereas oil from the rear camshaft bearing is forced upward through drillings in the cylinder block and the cylinder head to lubricate the overhead valve mechanism by means of the drilled rear rockershaft support and hollow rockershaft, which is cross-drilled where the valve rockers are located. The cylinders and pistons are lubricated by oil spraying out of an oil hole drilled in each connecting rod on the thrust side of the cylinders.

The fuel system employs an electrically-operated SU fuel pump, twin semi-downdraught SU carburettors, type HS4, and the fuel tank, which is situated in the rear of the vehicle.

In order to comply with government regulations in various countries concerning air pollution, later type engines (with serial number prefix 18GA) are equipped with a closed or positive crankcase ventilation system, consisting of a modified cylinder-block side plate with a built-in gauze filter. This filter serves as an oil-separator, which directs fluid oil particles back into the sump. A tube, welded to the side cover, is connected to a regulating device on the inlet manifold by means of a flexible hose. The system is equipped with a special oil filler cap on the valve-rocker cover; this filler cap has a built-in air-filter element, through which, via small holes in the cap, fresh air is drawn into the engine. After having circulated through the engine, the air is drawn out via the cylinder-block side cover and passes through the regulator valve assembly into the inlet manifold.

The amount of air which is drawn out by the engine vaccum is proportional to the engine speed and is governed to the pre-determined level by the regulator valve. The regulator valve is of the spring-assisted diaphragm type, which also serves as a check or non-return valve. The valve assembly, as well as the filter in the oil filler cap, should be cleaned at regular intervals; for details regarding this operation, refer to *Lubrication and Maintenance* in this manual.

**Description (Engine type 18GB):**

The engine of this type is basically similar to the engine described above; however, several important modifications have been made as outlined in the following description.

**Note: Changes in tolerances, dimensions and torque figures are specified under *Technical Data*. When carrying out repairs, or when reconditioning engine components, be sure to refer to the appropriate specification column in the back of this manual.**

Unlike the earlier types 18G and 18GA, the crankshaft of the 18GB type engine runs in five main bearings, which consist of replaceable steel-backed bearing shells lined with copper/lead bearing material. The bearing shells are available in standard size and four undersizes. The crankshaft thrust and the crankshaft end-float is taken at the centre main bearing by means of semi-circular thrust washers, similar to those as described for the early type engines. For the purpose of lubrication, the crankshaft is drilled so that each main bearing supplies its nearest connecting-rod bearing with oil.

The solid-skirt type pistons of this engine are fitted to the connecting rods by means of fully-floating piston pins kept in place by circlips in the piston-pin bore of the pistons; to this end, the closed connecting-rod upper ends are fitted with a replaceable bronze bush.

*Removal of the engine without the gearbox:*

(1) Drain the coolant and the engine oil and disconnect the battery terminals. Remove the bonnet, and if an oil-cooler is fitted, disconnect all the connections at the engine, the oil-filter and the oil-cooler itself. Detach the bracket supporting the oil-filter/oil-cooler connection at the generator.

(2) Remove the radiator and its mounting plate after having disconnected the necessary water hoses. Remove the air-cleaners and both carburettors, together with their interlinkage assembly.

(3) Detach the exhaust down-pipes from the flanges on the exhaust manifold and remove the heat deflector plate as well as the inlet and exhaust manifold.

(4) Disconnect the wiring and detach the ignition coil, together with its mounting bracket, from the front engine mounting; remove the oil-filter assembly and the starter motor.

(5) Disconnect and remove the thermal transmitter unit, the distributor cap with the high-tension leads, the oil pressure gauge union, the heater control cable, the heater hoses and the tachometer drive cable.

(6) Take the weight of the engine in a suitable tackle, which should be attached to the engine lifting lugs on the valve-rocker cover, and place a suitable stand underneath the gearbox. Remove the nuts securing the engine front mounting brackets to the rubber mountings and completely detach one mounting rubber from the chassis cross-member.

(7) Detach the rear engine mounting and remove the bolts securing the clutch bell-housing to the engine rear adaptor plate. Detach the exhaust down-pipe support bracket from the lower part of the clutch bell-housing. Make sure that all

necessary wiring, controls and connections are free for withdrawal of the engine.

(8) Carefully lift the assembly a little at a time, so that it can be pulled forward to clear the sump from the front cross-member and to disengage the gearbox input shaft or primary shaft from the clutch driven plate.

*Removal of the engine, together with the gearbox:*

Proceed as outlined under items 1 to and including 6 of the above paragraph and continue as follows:

(1) Drain the oil from the gearbox; disconnect and remove the propellor shaft and disconnect the speedometer drive cable at the gearbox.

(2) Detach the hydraulic clutch slave cylinder and temporarily tie it clear of the gearbox.

(3) Remove the bolts securing the rear cross-member to the chassis and allow the gearbox to settle on the fixed cross-member.

(4) Detach the engine stabilizer rod at the engine and remove the bolts securing the rear engine mounting to the gearbox; remove the rear cross-member together with the stabilizer rod.

(5) From the inside of the vehicle remove the gearshift lever and the rubber dust boot. Carefully ease the engine and gearbox assembly forward, so that the gearbox clears the cross-member; then tilt the gearbox and carefully lift the assembly out of the engine compartment.

*Dismantling and assembling of the engine (all types):*

*Dismantling:*

After the engine has been removed from the vehicle, the gearbox and clutch assembly must be removed, after which dismantling is effected as follows:

First, remove the remaining anciliary engine equipment, such as the ignition distributor, the water pump, the spark plugs etc.

Remove the valve-rocker cover and its gasket.

**Note: The four valve rockershaft support outer attachment stud nuts also serve as cylinder-head attachment stud nuts; as loosening or tightening cylinder-head stud nuts should always be done in the sequence specified by the manufacturer, the valve rockershaft support attaching stud nuts must not be loosened, unless all cylinder-head attaching nuts are loosened in the sequence given on page 25.**

Note the special locking plate under the right-hand rear rocker stud nut.

After having removed the valve rockershaft with the rockershaft supports and the valve rockers, the cylinder head may be carefully lifted from the studs. Remove and discard the cylinder-head gasket. Remove the pushrods and keep them in their relative positions to ensure replacement in their original bores.

After having removed the valve-keeper retaining clips and the valve-keepers with the aid of a suitable valve spring compressing tool, the valve spring upper retaining washers, the O-ring type valve stem oil-seals, the inner valve spring guides, the double valve springs and the valve spring lower seating washers can be removed, in that order.

On later engines, the O-ring type valve stem oil-seals are fitted between the valve-keepers and the valve spring upper retaining washers.

Gradually loosen the bolts securing the clutch assembly to the flywheel, in diagonal order, and remove the clutch assembly. Remove the flywheel attaching bolts and withdraw the flywheel, after having marked its position in relation to the crankshaft flange. Remove the engine rear adaptor plate securing bolts and withdraw the plate, together with its gasket. Remove the engine sump with its gasket and remove the oil pick-up strainer as well as the oil pump with its gasket. Remove the retaining bolt and extract the crankshaft pulley using a suitable extractor. Remove the timing-chain cover with its gasket and, if necessary, remove the neo-prene oil-seal from the cover in order to renew it.

Remove the camshaft sprocket retaining nut and remove the plug and the copper sealing washer from the bottom of the Reynolds-type chain-tensioner body. Insert an $\frac{1}{8}$ in hexagonal or Allen wrench into the plug hole and turn it in a clock-wise direction until the tensioner block is fully withdrawn from the timing chain. Remove the chain tensioner with its backing plate. Now both sprockets, together with the timing chain, should simultaneously be levered off their respective shafts with the aid of small levers or rigid screwdrivers. Take care not to lose or distort the adjustment shims situated behind the crankshaft sprocket. Remove the cam-shaft thrust flange and the front engine adaptor plate with its gasket. Remove the valve tappet covers with their gaskets and lift out the valve tappets, keeping them in the order of removal for identification when reassembling. Carefully withdraw the camshaft, taking care not to damage the camshaft bearing bushes. Mark the positions of the pistons, as well as the main and big-end bearing caps (if not already done), and remove the big-end bearing caps with the big-end bearing lower half shells. Push each piston and connecting-rod assembly up and out of the cylinder bores, after having removed the upper bearing half shells from the connecting rods. Be sure to keep the big-end bearing shells with their respective connecting rods, to ensure correct replacement.

Measure the crankshaft end-float and then remove the five main bearing caps with their half bearing shells and the two semi-circular thrust washers fitted on both sides of the centre main bearing cap.

Carefully lift out the crankshaft and remove the upper half main bearing shells and the remaining two semi-circular thrust washers from the cylinder block. With-draw the distributor drive-shaft by screwing a 5/16in UNF bolt into the threaded spindle in order to obtain a good grip. Remove the piston-pin pinch-bolts; mark the position of the pistons in relation to the connecting-rod, and push out the piston pins. Engines of type 18GB are equipped with pistons which are fitted to the connecting rods by means of a fully-floating piston pin, held in place with conven-tional circlips. It is essential to keep the piston pins with their respective pistons to ensure correct replacement. If necessary, remove the piston rings from the piston-ring grooves and meticulously clean out the grooves; keep each ring so that it can be replaced in its original groove on reassembly, if required.

Carefully clean and inspect all parts, replace all gaskets, lockwashers and pre-ferably the oil-seals.

*Reassembly:*

After having reconditioned the engine as necessary, reassembly is carried out as follows:

Install the piston rings in their respective grooves in the pistons and space the piston-ring gaps at 90 degrees to each other. Fit the connecting rods to the pistons by means of the piston pins. Early models employ a pinch-bolt in the connecting-rod upper end; later engines have a fully-floating piston pin which should be an easy thumb-fit into the piston at room temperature. The piston pins of these engines are secured with circlips. Lubricate the piston assemblies as well as the thoroughly-cleaned cylinder bores and fit the assemblies to the proper cylinder bores with the aid of a suitable piston-ring compressing tool. The open ends of the connecting-rod big-ends should be positioned towards the left-hand (camshaft) side of the engine. Do not push the assemblies all the way down into the cylinder bores but keep the piston crowns flush with the cylinder-head mating face. Place the cylinder block on its side or upside down and install the upper main bearing half-shells as well as the two upper semi-circular thrust washers, which must be fitted in the recesses machined in both sides of the main-bearing web. Apply some grease to prevent the washers dropping out of position. Note that the thrust washers should be fitted with their soft (lined) side facing the crankshaft flanks. Carefully place the crankshaft into the cylinder block, taking care not to dislodge the thrust washers. Install the lower main bearing half-shells in their respective bearing caps, ensuring that the locating tabs are properly seated in the machined recesses in the bearing-cap seatings.

Stick the lower thrust washer halves to the sides of the centre main-bearing cap with a little grease; fit all main-bearing caps, paying attention to the original markings, or those made during dismantling; tighten the nuts to the specified torque figure. Check that the crankshaft assembly rotates freely. Fit the upper connecting-rod bearing shells to the connecting rods; coat the shells with engine oil and push the pistons further down into the cylinder bores until the connecting rods, with their half-bearing shells, rest on the crankpin journals. Install the connecting-rod lower bearing shells in their respective bearing caps, paying attention to the original markings or those made when dismantling. After all bearing caps have been tightened to the correct torque (see *Technical Data*), ensure that the assembly can rotate freely. In order that dirt and dust can be kept out of the moving parts, it is advisable first to install the oil pump with the pick-up strainer, followed by the engine sump. Carefully insert the camshaft after having lubricated its bearing journals with engine oil; take care not to damage the camshaft bearing bushes in the cylinder block.

Lubricate the valve tappets and install these in the bores from which they were removed. New valve tappets are a selective fit; in lightly lubricated condition these should slide down their bores by their own weight. Install the valve push-rods in their respective positions. Fit the engine front mounting plate, using a new gasket and preferably a suitable gasket sealing compound. Fit the camshaft retaining flange with its three bolts and lockwashers.

Lubricate the valve guides with engine oil and fit the valves in their respective valve guides. Install the lower valve spring seating washers, the valve springs, the inner valve spring guides, new 'O'-ring type oil-seals on the valve stems, followed by the valve spring upper retaining washers. Compress the valve springs, using a suitable valve spring compressing tool, and install the valve-keepers followed by the valve-keeper retaining clips. Place a new cylinder-head gasket over the cylinder-head attaching studs, observing the stamped-in directions 'FRONT' and 'TOP'. Carefully lower the cylinder head onto the cylinder block and slip the heater hose support over the appropriate cylinder-head stud. Fit the stud nuts just finger-tight. Fit the special locking plate under the right-hand rear rocker stud nut. Install the valve rockershaft assembly and fit the nuts finger-tight. Tighten all stud nuts evenly to the specified torque in the sequence given below.

**Note: All valve rockershaft support outer attaching nuts are included in the cylinder-head stud nut tightening pattern: do not fail to observe this point or distortion and/or leakage will result.**

```
                    9    5    1    4    8
        front ─────────────────────────────
              10                          11
                    6    2    3    7
```

Tighten the remaining rockershaft support nuts evenly to the specified torque (see *Technical Data*).

Install the crankshaft timing-chain sprocket with the adjustment shims and the camshaft timing-chain sprocket. Push the crankshaft as well as the camshaft toward the rear of the engine to eliminate end-float and check the alignment of the sprocket-wheel teeth in relation to one another; this can be done with a straight-edge. Any discrepancy in the alignment must be corrected by adding or removing shims behind the crankshaft timing sprocket. Turn the crankshaft until the Woodruff key-way is exactly at T.D.C.; now turn the camshaft until its key-way is approximately in the 'one o'clock' position.

Place both sprockets in the timing chain with the markings on their front faces turned towards each other; fit this assembly onto the respective shafts and see that the markings are facing each other whilst coinciding with the centre-line through both shafts. It may be necessary to rotate the camshaft a fraction of a turn in order to align the key-way more accurately. Secure the camshaft sprocket with the locking washer and the retaining nut.

Install the timing-chain tensioner unit after having fully retracted the friction block by turning its plunger in a clockwise direction by means of an Allen key; once installed, turn the hexagonal plunger in a clockwise direction until the friction block tensions the chain by means of the built-in spring.

**Never turn the hexagonal plunger in an anti-clockwise direction in an attempt to further tension the chain.**

Slide the oil thrower ring, with its concave side (or the side marked 'F' on later engines), outwards, onto the crankshaft. If the special tool for centralization of the timing-chain cover oil-seal is not available, centralization may be done with the hub of the crankshaft pulley. Insert the lubricated pulley boss in the seal with a turning movement and place the cover with the centralizing tool (or pulley), and with a new gasket, onto the crankshaft. Gradually tighten the timing cover attachment bolts.

Install the engine rear adaptor plate, using a new gasket; install a new sealing strip. Evenly tighten the bolts to the specified torque. Install the flywheel, paying attention to the markings made when dismantling, and secure it with the locking plate and the six bolts. Install the clutch assembly, tightening the clutch-cover securing bolts evenly and to the specified torque figure: during this operation the clutch driven plate should be centralized; to this end, an old primary drive-shaft can be used. After the clutch-cover securing bolts have been tightened to the requisite torque, the centralizing tool can be withdrawn.

Further assembly is a reversal of the dismantling procedure; the ancillary engine components are dealt with elsewhere in this description. After installation in the vehicle, fill the cooling system with water to which an anti-corrosive additive or anti-freeze solution is added, and fill the engine and gearbox with the recommended lubricant. Valve clearances should be adjusted with the engine at operating temperature.

**Detailed description of reconditioning and servicing of engine components:**

**Cylinder head:**

**Note: If only the valve rockershaft is to be removed, note that all cylinder-head nuts must be loosened in the proper sequence (see page 25). It is therefore essential that the cooling system be drained before removal of the valve rockershaft.**

To dismantle the valve rockershaft, withdraw the split-pins, the flat washers and the spring washers from the ends of the shaft; remove the locating screw in the rear rocker support and slide the rockers, rocker supports and springs from the shaft.

Remove the plug from the forward end of the rockershaft and clean out the oilway. Replacing valve rocker bushes should be carried out with service tool 18G226. Bushes and rockers are very easily ruined by using improvised drifts. When pressing-in new bushes, take care to drill the oil holes so that they coincide with the oil drillings in the valve rockers. The oil groove must be at the bottom of the rocker bore. Ream the bushes to the dimensions as given in *Technical Data*.

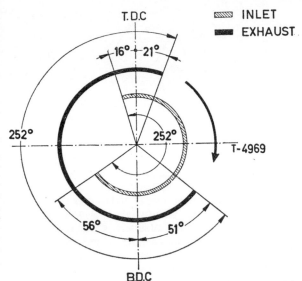

**Fig. 14. Valve timing diagram**

When new valve guides are to be pressed in, the old guides must be pressed out toward the combustion chamber. The new guides should then be pressed in toward the combustion chamber until the chamfered top part of each guide projects above the valve spring seat on the cylinder head by $\frac{3}{8}$ in for both inlet and exhaust. Press in inlet valve guides with the largest chamfer at the top; the counter-bored ends of the exhaust valve guides should face the combustion chambers. After pressing in new guides, the valve seats should be re-machined in order to centralize them in relation to the new valve guide bores. When installing the valves, be sure to renew the 'O'-ring type valve stem oil-seals; the re-use of old seals may lead to heavy oil consumption.

**Sump:** The sump can be removed without removing the engine from the car. Drain the radiator, disconnect the hoses, drain the sump and release the front engine mounting bolts.

Lift the engine sufficiently to gain access to the bolts, remove the crankcase-to-sump bolts and withdraw the sump.

Reinstallation is a direct reversal of the removal procedure.

**Camshaft bearings:** If necessary, the camshaft bearings can be replaced. This operation necessitates the use of service tools 18G124A, –B, –C, –F, –G, and –H. When installing new bearings, be sure to keep the oil holes in line with the oil drillings in the ground bores in the cylinder block. After installation of new bearing bushes, these should be reamed-out with the special reamer set 18G123A and the adaptors 18G123B, –E, –F, –L, –T, –AB, –AC, –AD.

**Valve timing:** The valve timing should be checked with a valve clearance of 0·021 in; after checking the valve timing, be sure to re-adjust the valves to their normal working clearance.

**Starter ring gear:** If the starter ring gear should need replacement, it can be removed by splitting the gear between two teeth with the aid of a cold chisel; to facilitate this, a small hole may be drilled through the ring gear in order to perforate it, after

c

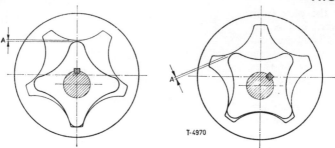

**Fig. 15. Oil pump rotors**                          A = 0.006 in.

which the final break may be done with the chisel. Make sure that the new ring gear and its seating on the flywheel are perfectly clean and free from burrs. Heat the ring gear to a temperature of 300 to 400°C (570–752°F); at this temperature the colour of the ring gear turns to light blue. Do not exceed this limit or the temper of the teeth will be affected adversely. Quickly place the heated ring gear squarely onto its seating with the chamfer of the teeth towards the flywheel boss; upon cooling down, the ring gear will be a natural shrink-fit on its seating, making any additional securing superfluous.

**Oil pump:** After removal of the oil pump the rotor end-float and radial clearance can be checked.

Place a straight-edge across the top face of the pump body. Measure the gap between the rotor upper face and the straight-edge; this should not exceed 0·005 in. The pump body face may be carefully lapped to remedy excessive clearance.

The clearances between the lobes can be measured with the aid of feeler gauges in the positions shown in Fig. 15. The clearances should not exceed 0·006 in.

When reassembling the pump, take care that the outer rotor is installed with the chamfered end facing the driving side.

**Ignition:** Ignition by battery, coil and ignition distributor. The distributor is equipped with centrifugal and vacuum advance mechanism. After having removed the distributor cap with the high-tension cables and having disconnected the low-tension lead, the distributor can be withdrawn by removing the two retaining screws. The distributor drive spindle can easily be withdrawn by screwing a 5/16 in UNF bolt into the tapped hole of the spindle. Before installing the distributor, set piston No.1 at T.D.C. (compr.) by aligning the notch in the crankshaft pulley outer flange with the longest pointer on the timing cover. Hold the drive spindle with the slot in a horizontal position, the larger off-set uppermost, above the bore in the cylinder block. As the helical drive gears mesh, the spindle will turn anti-clockwise until its slot is approximately in the two o'clock position. Install the distributor, secure it with the two attaching bolts, and slacken the pinch-bolt. Turn the crankshaft approximately 90° in counter-clockwise direction, then slowly turn it clockwise, until the notch in the crankshaft pulley outer flange coincides with the nearest pointer on the timing cover to the required setting. The longest pointer indicates T.D.C., the next 5° B.T.D.C. and the last 10° B.T.D.C.

Connect the low-tension distributor lead and the vacuum line; connect a 12-volt test lamp between the low-tension terminal on the distributor and earth. Turn the knurled vernier adjustment nut on the distributor housing, opposite the vacuum advance unit, until the scale protrudes half-way. Install the rotor, the tip of which should be pointing towards the spark plug segment for No. 1 cylinder, inside the distributor cap. Switch on the ignition and slowly turn the distributor counter-clockwise until the contact points fully close and consequently the test lamp goes out; now slowly turn the distributor housing clockwise until the contact points just commence to open and the test lamp just lights up. In this position secure the distributor by tightening the pinch-bolt. Do not forget to switch off the ignition.

The setting can afterwards be altered to some degree by turning the knurled vernier adjustment nut; the markings 'A' and 'R' on the distributor housing, adjacent to the nut, stand for Advance and Retard respectively. Each graduation equals approximately 5° alteration (crankshaft degrees) of the ignition timing setting and 11 'clicks' of the adjustment nut will change the setting by one degree.

It is advisable to check the aforementioned adjustment with the aid of a neon timing light, bearing in mind that in this case the timing should be 3° B.T.D.C. at 600 rpm.

**Fuel pump:** The electrical SU fuel pump is situated on a bracket just beside the front mounting point of the left-hand rear road spring and can be reached from underneath the car. On earlier type cars the SU type HP and on later type cars the SU type AUF 300 fuel pump is fitted.

*Removal and installation:*

Disconnect the battery earth terminal and the electrical connections at the fuel pump.

Disconnect the fuel pump inlet and outlet unions and remove the two bolts securing the fuel-pump mounting bracket to the underbody.

Installation is a direct reversal of the removal procedure.

*Dismantling:*

NOTE: Before dismantling the fuel pump, its exterior should be cleaned thoroughly to avoid contamination of the vital parts.

First remove the insulating sleeve, the terminal nut and the connector with its shake-proof washer. Remove the end-cover, after having removed the tape seal (if fitted). Remove the 5BA screw holding the contact blade to the support plate, and ease the condenser from its retaining clamp. Remove the support washer, the long coil wire and the contact point.

*Coil housing and diaphragm:*

Remove the two coil-housing securing screws, using a thick-bladed screwdriver to prevent damage to the screw heads. Remove the earthing screw from the housing, after which the coil housing can be removed. Next remove the diaphragm and the spindle by turning the diaphragm anti-clockwise until the spring tension pushes the diaphragm away from the coil housing, taking care not to lose the 11 brass centralizing rollers. The diaphragm and its spindle form one unit and should not be replaced separately.

*Support plate and rocker mechanism:*

Remove the terminal nut from the support plate, followed by the lead washer, which in most cases must be cut to allow removal. Remove the support plate-to-coil housing securing screws and remove the earth terminal tags and the condenser retaining clamp. Tilt the support plate and withdraw the terminal stud from the tag. The support plate, together with the rocker mechanism, may now be removed. Gently tap or push the hardened steel pivot pin, attaching the rocker mechanism, from its bores in the support plate.

*Fuel-pump housing and valves (pump type AUF 300):*

Remove the two retaining plate securing screws and remove the valve covers, the valves, the sealing washers and the filter.

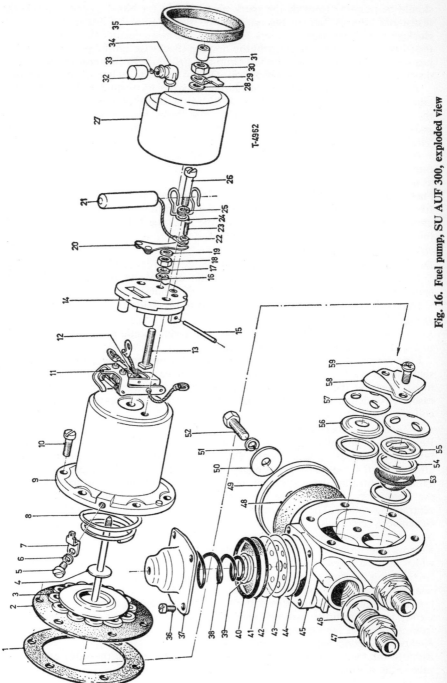

T-4952

**Fig. 16. Fuel pump, SU AUF 300, exploded view**

**Note: Do not dismantle the delivery flow smoothing device unless its operation is faulty, and equipment is available for pressure testing after reassembly. If so, proceed as follows:**

Remove the four BA screws securing the vent cover of the mechanism and remove the cover, the diaphragm spring, the rubber washers, the spacer, the diaphragm disc and the sealing ring, in that order.

Remove the two BA screws securing the air inlet cover, and remove the cover and its gasket. Remove the inlet and outlet unions.

*Fuel-pump housing and valves (type HP):*

Remove the inlet and outlet union and remove the housing of the outlet valve and the inlet valve disc. Remove the lower plug and the filter.

**Inspection:**

*General:*

Those components of the fuel pump which have been in contact with gum formation in the fuel, become coated with a substance similar to varnish; these deposits will eventually lead to destruction of the neoprene pump diaphragm, so that it is of utmost importance that all components be thoroughly checked and cleaned. If an unpleasant stale smell is noticed around the outlet union, it indicates that gum formation is present. The ordinary, sharp, acrid smell of petrol indicates an absence of gum formation.

Any brass or steel parts of the fuel pump which have been contaminated with gum should be boiled in 20 per cent caustic soda solution, immersed in strong nitric acid and then washed in boiling water. Those parts made of aluminium should be thoroughly soaked in methylated spirits and cleaned afterwards.

*Fuel pump, type HP:*

Carefully clean the pump housing and inspect for cracks, damaged jointing faces and defective threads.

Carefully clean the filter with a stiff brush and examine its condition; when in doubt, always replace the filter.

Check the condition of the contact breaker points; if they are burned, the rocker mechanism should be replaced as a unit.

Check the condition of the pump diaphragm. Examine the condition of the check valve in the cover and ensure that the valve ball is free to move.

| | | |
|---|---|---|
| *Key to Fig.* 16: | 20 Contact blade | 40 Rubber sealing ring |
| 1 Gasket | 21 Condenser | 41 Rubber diaphragm |
| 2 Diaphragm | 22 Washer | 42 Plastic diaphragm backing plate |
| 3 Brass rollers | 23 Set-screw | 43 Diaphragm backing plate |
| 4 Abutment collar | 24 Condenser retainer | 44 Sealing ring |
| 5 Set-screw | 25 Spring washer | 45 Pump housing |
| 6 Washer | 26 Support plate set-screw | 46 Sealing washer |
| 7 Male earth connector | 27 Cover | 47 Outlet union |
| 8 Diaphragm spring | 28 Washer | 48 Gasket |
| 9 Coil housing | 29 Male connector | 49 Air inlet cover |
| 10 Coil housing screw | 30 Terminal nut | 50 Washer |
| 11 Rocker mechanism | 31 Insulating sleeve | 51 Lock washer |
| 12 Trunnion | 32 ⎤ | 52 Set-screw |
| 13 Terminal stud | 33 ⎬ Bleeder valve assembly | 53 Filter |
| 14 Rocker support plate | 34 ⎦ | 54 Sealing washer |
| 15 Pivot pin | 35 Dust band | 55 Inlet valve |
| 16 Washer | 36 Set-screw | 56 Outlet valve |
| 17 Lead washer | 37 Cover | 57 Valve seat |
| 18 Nut | 38 Diaphragm spring | 58 Valve retaining plate |
| 19 Washer | 39 Spring seating washer | 59 Set-screw for 58 |

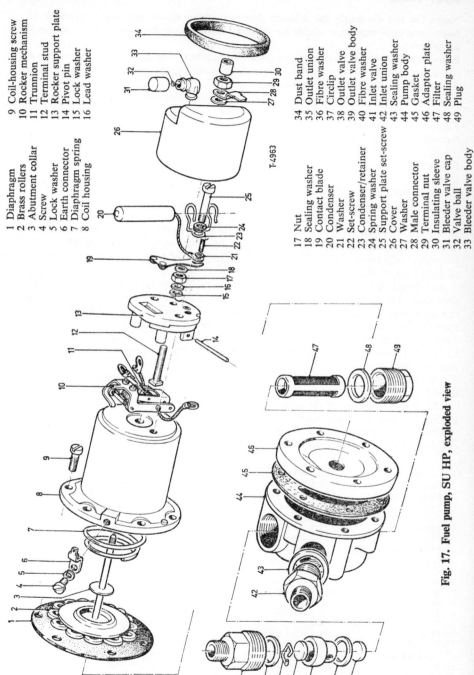

1 Diaphragm
2 Brass rollers
3 Abutment collar
4 Screw
5 Lock washer
6 Earth connector
7 Diaphragm spring
8 Coil housing
9 Coil-housing screw
10 Rocker mechanism
11 Trunnion
12 Terminal stud
13 Rocker support plate
14 Pivot pin
15 Lock washer
16 Lead washer

17 Nut
18 Sealing washer
19 Contact blade
20 Condenser
21 Washer
22 Set-screw
23 Condenser/retainer
24 Spring washer
25 Support plate set-screw
26 Cover
27 Washer
28 Male connector
29 Terminal nut
30 Insulating sleeve
31 Bleeder valve cap
32 Valve ball
33 Bleeder valve body

34 Dust band
35 Outlet union
36 Fibre washer
37 Circlip
38 Outlet valve
39 Outlet valve body
40 Fibre washer
41 Inlet union
42 Inlet valve
43 Sealing washer
44 Pump body
45 Gasket
46 Adaptor plate
47 Filter
48 Sealing washer
49 Plug

T-4963

Fig. 17. Fuel pump, SU HP, exploded view

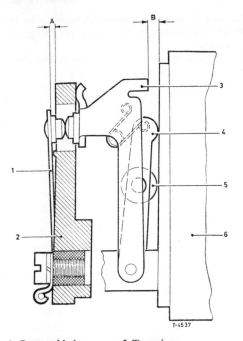

1 Contact blade    5 Trunnion
2 Support plate    6 Coil housing
3 Outer rocker    A = 0·035 in
4 Inner rocker    B = 0·070 in

Fig. 18. SU fuel pump rocker mechanism, sectioned view

*Fuel pump, type AUF 300:*

Examine the plastic valve assemblies for distortion, wear or damage; this can best be done by blowing and sucking with the mouth. Check that the valve retaining tab is positioned so that the valve is properly retained in its recess but is allowed a lift of approximately $\frac{1}{16}$ in. If the valve seats are pitted, the pump body must be replaced.

Check that the coil-housing vent is unobstructed. Carefully examine the general condition of the rocker mechanism, replacing those parts that show signs of wear, damage or distortion.

The following parts should always be replaced:

Fibre and cork washers, gaskets and 'O'-ring type seals, worn or damaged rollers, damaged bolts and unions.

**Assembly:**
*Support plate and rocker mechanism:*
**Note: The hardened steel pivot pin securing the rocker assembly to the support plate should be replaced only by a genuine SU part.**

Place the support plate upside down and attach the rocker assembly by means of the hardened steel pivot pin. Position the centre toggle so that when the inner rocker spindle is tensioned against the rear of the contact point the centre toggle spring is above the spindle on which the white rollers run.

The importance of a completely free-moving rocker mechanism cannot be over-emphasized; any bent parts should be straightened with suitable needle-nosed pliers.

Further assembly of the rocker mechanism is a reversal of the dismantling procedure; the contact blade, however, should not be installed at this stage. The support plate retaining screws must not be over-tightened, or damaged to the plate will result.

*Diaphragm:*
Place the diaphragm spring, large diameter first, into the housing. Before fitting the diaphragm, make sure the small neoprene washer is fitted into the armature recess. The diaphragm should not be installed with jointing compound of any sort. Install the diaphragm assembly and screw its spindle into the threaded centre rocker trunnion, until the rocker will not throw over.

Install the eleven brass rollers by turning up the diaphragm-edge and dropping the rollers into the coil recess; during this operation, the pump should be held with the rocker end downwards, thus preventing the rollers from dropping out.

**Note: On later type rockers with adjustable fingers, the contact blade must be installed at this stage and the fingers adjusted as described in the appropriate paragraph in this manual; then remove the contact blade.**

Firmly push the diaphragm spindle whilst unscrewing the diaphragm and pushing intermittently until the rocker just 'throws-over'; now unscrew the diaphragm until the holes in the diaphragm edge line-up with the next nearest holes in the pump housing and then another four holes further; this procedure gives the proper diaphragm adjustment.

To prevent the rollers dropping out, press the centre of the armature and insert the retaining fork (SU tool) at the rear of the rocker mechanism.

*Assembling the pump housing (pump type AUF 300):*

The recess for the inlet valve assembly in the housing is deeper than the recess for the outlet valve, thus providing room for the filter and the sealing ring. Tighten the inlet and outlet unions with the sealing rings. Install the outlet valve components into the recess as follows: the sealing ring, the valve (tab facing downwards) and the valve cover.

Install the inlet valve components in the recess in the following order: sealing ring, filter (round part facing down), and the sealing ring, the valve (with its tab turned upwards) and finally the valve cover.

Install the valve retaining plate and secure with the two screws.

Install the air inlet cover with the sealing ring and secure with the central retaining screw.

Install the sealing ring into the bottom of the recess for the fuel supply smoothing device, followed by the perforated diaphragm plate (round side facing downwards); then install the plastic disc, followed by the rubber diaphragm. Install the sealing ring into the recess and ensure that it is properly seated. Install the diaphragm spring (wide end facing the cover) into the cover; place the spring seating washer onto the small end of the spring and insert the special assembly tool through the cover, the spring and the spring seating washer. Turn the tool by 90° and tension the spring; then fit the cover and the spring to the diaphragm. Tighten the four securing screws and remove the tool. After assembly the unit must be pressure-tested with the aid of special equipment.

*Assembling the pump housing (pump type HP):*

Install the brass disc of the outlet valve on the housing and ensure that the plain side of the disc is facing the valve seat; secure the disc by installing the retaining clip into the groove. When the valve housing is shaken, the valve must be heard to rattle freely.

Drop the inlet valve disc, plain side down, into the housing; install the thin fibre washer and drop the outlet valve housing into position, after which the thicker fibre washer should be installed.

Next tighten the outlet union with the aid of a suitable spanner.

Install the inlet union and the filter.

*Installing the pump housing (pump type AUF 300):*

Place the sealing ring on the housing, align the securing hole and place the coil housing in position; ensure that the jointing faces meet properly. Align the six securing screw holes; the cast tabs on the coil housing must be positioned downwards. Install the six securing screws and do not forget the earthing screw and the Lucar connector.

Remove the brass roller retaining fork carefully, ensuring that the rollers remain in position; otherwise the diaphragm may be damaged.

Tighten the securing screws in a diagonal pattern.

*Installing the pump housing (pump type HP):*
Install the gasket and the intermediate plate onto the housing; the concave side of the plate must be facing the diaphragm. Align the securing holes and place the coil housing, ensuring that the jointing faces meet properly. Ensure that the unions are on top and the filter on the bottom of the housing.

Align the securing holes and ensure that the cast tabs on the coil housing are at the bottom. Install the six securing screws and do not forget the earthing screw and the Lucar connector.

Remove the brass roller retaining fork carefully, ensuring that the rollers are not dislodged; otherwise the diaphragm may be damaged.

Tighten the securing screws in a diagonal pattern.

*Contact blade:*
Install the contact blade and the coil lead to the support plate with the 5 BA washer and the screw. Place the mounting tab of the condenser beneath the coil lead terminal.

Adjust the contact blade so that when closed the contact points are a fraction above the rocker points when closed, and that one set of points wipe across the centre-line of the other in a symmetrical manner when the contact points just commence to open or close.

Some degree of adjustment is possible by means of the slotted securing hole in the contact blade.

Make sure that when the outer rocker is pressed toward the coil housing the contact blade rests on the narrow rib projecting above the main face of the support plate; if this is not the case, swing the blade clear of the support plate and bend it downward, so that when installed, it rests lightly against the rib. Do not over-tension the blade.

*Rocker mechanism (modified type):*
With the aid of a feeler gauge, check the gap produced by the lift of the contact blade above the top of the support plate; if necessary, the stop-finger can be bent in order to obtain the requisite gap of $0 \cdot 035 \pm 0 \cdot 005$ in. Measure the gap between the rocker finger and the coil housing; if necessary, the stop can be bent to obtain the requisite gap of $0 \cdot 070 \pm 0 \cdot 005$ in.

*Rocker mechanism (earlier type):*
Check the gap between the contact points in an indirect manner, by carefully pressing the contact blade against the rib or edge on the support plate without pressing on the point; the gap thus formed between the white rollers and the housing should be $0 \cdot 030$ in. If necessary, the point of the contact blade can be adjusted to give the requisite gap.

Further assembly of the fuel pump is a reversal of the dismantling procedure.

**Carburettors:** Make: S U, type HS4.

**General:**
S U carburettors are of the variable choke type; the fuel is metered by means of a tapered needle in the jet. The needle is secured to the sleeve, which determines the amount of throttle opening; the position of the sleeve and the needle are in turn determined by the vacuum piston (the upper part of the sleeve), in accordance with the throttle opening. In Fig. 19B a schematic view of the construction is shown. Normally the piston, the sleeve and the needle are in the lowest position when the throttle is closed, but for clarity these parts are shown in a slightly raised position. The piston is a free fit in the vacuum chamber with a very small clearance. A guide spindle is centrally located in the piston; this spindle is free to move up and down

1 Piston damper
2 Sealing washer
3 Vacuum chamber
4 Piston spring
5 Vacuum piston with guide spindle
6 Jet needle locating screw
7 Jet needle
8 Piston guide key
9 Carburettor body
10 Jet retainer
11 Sealing washer
12 Jet retainer screw
13 Spring
14 Jet adjusting nut
15 Jet assembly
16 Throttle jet interconnecting link
17 Carburettor coupling assembly
18 Throttle assembly
19 Idle speed adjusting screw
20 Lift pin assembly
21 Float chamber attaching bolt
22 Adaptor
23 Special washer
24 Float chamber

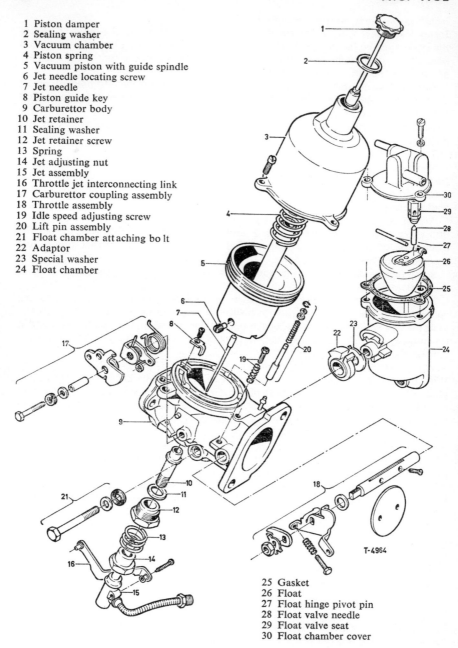

T-4964

25 Gasket
26 Float
27 Float hinge pivot pin
28 Float valve needle
29 Float valve seat
30 Float chamber cover

**Fig. 19A. Carburettor, SU HS4, exploded view**

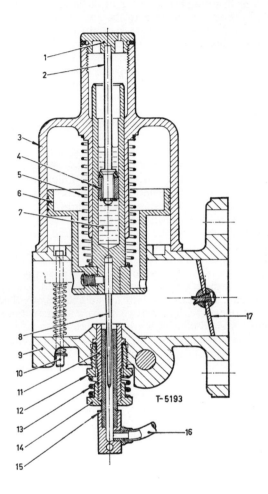

**Fig. 19B. Carburettor, schematic view (HS, typical)**

1 Damper piston cap
2 Damper piston stem
3 Vacuum chamber
4 Damper piston assembly
5 Vacuum piston assist spring
6 Vacuum piston assembly
7 Damper oil reservoir
8 Jet needle
9 Carburettor body
10 Piston lifting pin
11 Jet retainer
12 Jet retainer nut
13 Spring
14 Jet adjusting nut
15 Jet assembly
16 Fuel line
17 Throttle valve

in the guide bore of the vacuum chamber, thus ensuring correct alignment of the piston and vacuum chamber at all times. When the engine is not running, the piston and the needle assembly will fall to the bottom by their own weight and by the tension of the assist spring fitted on top of the vacuum piston. With the engine running, the sleeve forms a restriction to the airstream, thus a partial vacuum is created. This pressure drop also creates a partial vacuum in the vacuum chamber above the piston, causing the piston, the sleeve and the needle to rise a certain amount. The raised needle determines the amount of fuel emerging from the jet; thus the correct air/fuel mixture is automatically established. When starting a cold engine, the mixture may be enriched by pulling down the jet; the mouth of the jet will now be in line with a thinner portion of the needle, thus supplying a richer mixture. The jet is mounted in a jet retainer bush and is fed with fuel by a small flexible nylon tube connected to the base of the float chamber.

*Fitting jet needles and centralizing the jets:*
When fitting the needle, the position of the needle should be as shown in Fig. 20. During assembly of the carburettor, it is imperative to ensure that the jet and needle are correctly centralized. To check this, proceed as follows:

Unscrew the union of the small nylon tube at the bottom of the float chamber; unscrew the jet adjusting nut and carefully withdraw the jet, together with the adjusting nut and spring, downwards from the carburettor housing. Remove the spring and re-insert the jet into the retainer bush and temporarily connect the nylon tube to the float chamber; loosen the jet retainer nut and screw the jet adjusting nut all the way up. Remove the piston damper assembly from the vacuum chamber and carefully and gently push down on the piston guide spindle; tighten the jet retainer nut. Lift the piston and release it; it should now fall to the bottom of the carburettor bore (the bridge) with an audible 'click'. Turn down the jet adjusting nut about one-and-a-half or two turns and again raise the piston and let it fall. The piston should contact the bridge with an audible 'click' as before.

Remove the jet and adjusting nut, install the spring and reinstall the complete jet with spring and adjustment nut, this time firmly connecting the nylon tube to the float chamber. Make sure that the tube projects about $\frac{3}{16}$-in beyond the rubber sealing ring.

Screw the jet adjustment nut up as far as it will go, then turn it down by approximately two full turns for initial setting. Re-check that the piston and needle assembly will fall freely, then refit the damper assembly, after having filled the damper spindle to the top of its bore with SAE20 oil.

*Float settings:*
Remove the float chamber cover and float assembly, and hold it inverted in a horizontal position. When the float setting is correct, a round bar of $\frac{3}{16}$-in diameter will just fit between the float arm and the edge on the float chamber cover. If necessary, the float setting may be corrected by carefully bending the cranked portion of the float arm.

*Carburettor adjustments:*
Make sure that the vacuum chamber and the piston are clean, the needle properly fitted and the jet correctly centralized. Check the damper for correct oil level and top-up if necessary, then proceed as follows:
(1) Ensure that the idle adjustment screws are holding the throttle valves partially open and that the jet adjustment screws are not screwed all the way up. (An average setting to start with is obtained by turning each idle adjustment screw down one full turn from the fully closed position of the throttle valve and the

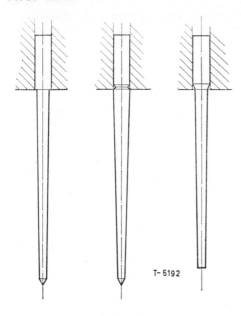

Fig. 20. Carburettor jet needles

T-5192

jet adjusting nut one-and-a-half to two turns down from the top position.)

(2) Make sure that the jet is firmly against the adjustment nut; if necessary, readjust or disconnect the choke cable.

(3) Warm-up the engine and set the throttle to an idling speed of approximately 700 rpm. Check the mixture of each carburettor in turn by lifting the piston approximately 1/32 in by means of the spring-loaded piston lifting pin. If, when the piston is lifted, the engine speed increases, the mixture is too rich and the jet adjusting nut must be screwed up by one-sixth of a turn at a time until the desired result is obtained; if, on the other hand, the engine speed decreases, the mixture is too lean and the jet adjusting nut must consequently be screwed down by one-sixth of a turn at a time.

(4) Continue adjusting the carburettors until, when either piston is lifted, the engine speed increases momentarily, very slightly. The mixture is then correctly set and the engine beat should be smooth and regular.

(5) Reconnect and adjust the choke cable, to ensure that it has $\frac{1}{16}$ in slack before it commences to operate the jet lever. Pull out the choke control on the facia by approximately $\frac{5}{8}$ in (until the jet is just about to be pulled down), and turn the fast idle adjusting screws until an engine speed of about 1000 rpm is obtained.

(6) Push in the choke control as far as it will go and check whether there is a small clearance between each fast-idle screw tip and its abutment; the clearance at this point should be about 1/64 in.

(7) Finally, re-check the idle speed and mixture.

*Synchronizing the carburettors:*

If a special device for synchronization of the carburettors is not available, an adequate result may be obtained with a suitable small-diameter rubber hose. The synchronizing procedure is as follows:

Disconnect the throttle shaft coupling to ensure that the throttle shaft of each carburettor can move independently. Turn both idle adjustment screws so that both throttles are just completely closed, then open each throttle by about one full turn of each screw. Start and warm-up the engine and turn each screw an equal amount until a satisfactory idle speed is obtained. Holding one end of the rubber hose to the ear and the other end near the carburettor air intake, a hissing sound will be noticed. Note the intensity of the hiss and move the rubber hose to the air intake of the second carburettor, holding it in exactly the same position. Adjust the throttle screws until both carburettors produce a hissing sound of equal intensity, then re-connect the throttle shaft coupling.

**Water pump:** A water pump of the impeller type is mounted to the front end of the cylinder block by means of four attachment bolts. With the engine *in situ* it is possible to remove the water pump after removing the radiator.

*Dismantling:*

After removal, the water pump can be dismantled as follows:

First remove the four securing bolts and withdraw the fan and pulley assembly from the hub. Remove the pulley flange with a suitable extractor.

Remove the bearing retaining wire from the hole in the top part of the pump body.

Gently tap the spindle rearward and withdraw the assembly from the pump body. Withdraw the vane from the spindle, using a suitable extractor.

Carefully clean and inspect all parts; renew the seal. Reassembly is effected in reverse order of the dismantling procedure, noting the following:

Before pressing-in the spindle with the bearing in position, make sure that the hole in the bearing is in line with the lubrication hole in the pump body. By pressing the impeller onto the spindle, note that the clearance between the vane and the pump body should be $0 \cdot 020$ to $0 \cdot 030$ in.

## TRANSMISSION

**Clutch:** Hydraulically-operated single dry-plate clutch of the diaphragm-spring type. The clutch driven plate is connected to a splined hub by means of damper springs to absorb vibration. The annular friction linings are riveted to the clutch plate. The diaphragm clutch spring is fitted between two annular rings, which serve as pivot edge for the diaphragm spring when the clutch is operated. These rings and the diaphragm spring are attached to the clutch housing by means of nine equally spaced rivets. The clutch pressure plate is attached to the clutch housing by means of three laminated drive straps, which prevent the pressure plate assembly from turning relative to the clutch housing. At the clutch pressure plate ends these drive straps are secured by bolts; at the other end, the straps are secured by bolts and nuts.

The clutch release bearing consists of a graphite thrust ring, which protrudes from a steel housing. The release bearing is attached to the operating fork by means of two spring retainers. The clutch is a dynamically balanced unit; it is therefore not recommended to recondition the clutch driven plate. A clutch driven plate with oil-fouled or worn linings should be replaced complete.

*Removal of the clutch:*

Remove the engine as described. Loosen the bolts securing the clutch assembly to the flywheel by slackening them a turn at a time in a diagonal pattern, until the spring pressure is released. The clutch cover plate can now be removed from the dowels on the flywheel.

*Installation:*

Installation is a reversal of the removal procedure.

*Dismantling:*

Remove the circlip attaching the release plate to the diaphragm spring, and remove the plate.

Slacken the three bolts securing the clamps to the clutch pressure plate until the diaphragm spring touches the clutch housing. Remove the screws, the clamps, the washers and the pressure plate. Rotate the clutch release bearing retaining clips through 90° and remove the release bearing.

*Assembling:*

Assembly is a reversal of the dismantling procedure. Note that the clutch driven plate should be installed so that the large end of the hub is towards the gearbox. When

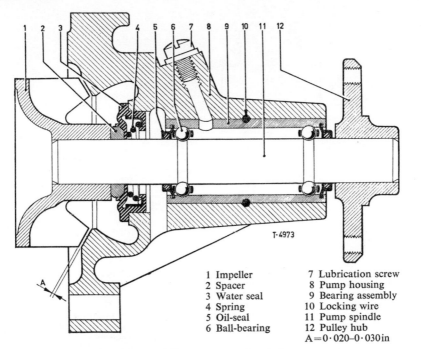

1 Impeller
2 Spacer
3 Water seal
4 Spring
5 Oil-seal
6 Ball-bearing
7 Lubrication screw
8 Pump housing
9 Bearing assembly
10 Locking wire
11 Pump spindle
12 Pulley hub
A=0·020–0·030 in

**Fig. 21. Water pump, sectioned view**

installing the clutch cover plate, the clutch driven plate should be centralized with a spare primary drive shaft (if no special tool is available). Do not remove the centralizing tool until all clutch securing bolts have been tightened to the requisite torque, given in *Technical Data.*

**Gearbox:** Four-speed gearbox with centrally-mounted gearshift lever. The top, third and second gears are synchronized by means of a baulk ring-type synchromesh system. Top gear is a direct drive, whereas the third- and second-speed pinions on the mainshaft and on the secondary shaft are in constant mesh. First and reverse gear are of the sliding mesh type with straight spur-type teeth. A combined filler plug and oil-level dipstick is located on top of the gearbox housing. The clutch unit and the starter motor drive are accommodated in the clutch bell-housing, which is part of the gearbox housing. The shifting mechanism is situated in a separate housing which is bolted to the rear end of the gearbox housing. At its front end, the gearbox is secured to the engine rear adaptor plate by means of bolts, while the rear end is mounted on the rear cross-member by means of two rubber mountings. The rear end of the gearbox is also connected to the rear cross-member by means of a reaction or stabilizer rod.

A Laycock de Normanville overdrive, operating on third and top gear, is available as an optional extra.

*Removal from the vehicle:*

Removal of the gearbox alone is not possible. For removal it is necessary to remove the engine and gearbox as a unit, after which the two components can be separated.

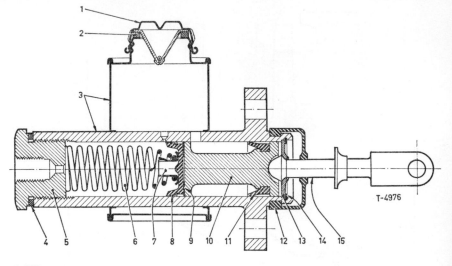

1 Filler cup
2 Sealing washer
3 Cylinder body
4 Sealing ring
5 Adaptor plug

6 Piston return spring
7 Spring guide
8 Cup
9 Backing washer
10 Piston

11 Secondary cup
12 Dust boot
13 Push-rod abutment washer
14 Circlip
15 Push-rod

**Fig. 22. Clutch master cylinder, sectioned view**

The removal procedure is outlined on page 23 of this manual.
*Installation:*
Installation is a reversal of the removal operations.
*Dismantling:*
(1) Remove the oil dipstick, the drain plug and the speedometer drive. With the aid of tool 18 G 2 extract the drive flange from the mainshaft.
(2) Remove the shifter-housing, the extension housing side cover and the interlock plate and bracket. Slacken the locating screw on the remote control front selector lever, remove the bolts and nuts securing the extension housing to the gearbox and remove the extension housing. Retain the remote control selector lever, which comes free as the extension housing is being removed.
(3) Remove the shaft and the rear selector lever from the rear extension and remove the selector lever from the shaft; withdraw the split bush and the circlip from the selector. Remove the three screws with countersunk heads, as well as the seven hexagon-headed screws securing the gearbox side cover, and remove the cover.
(4) Cut the locking wire and loosen the three selector/shifting dog locating screws; remove the dogs. Remove the shifter-fork shaft guide block, taking care to retain the three detent balls and springs, which are freed when taking the guide block from the shafts. Remove the two locating dowels.
   Remove the locking nuts, bolts and the serrated washers securing the shifter forks. Withdraw the shifter forks in the following order:
   Reverse gear, third/top gear, first/second gear. If the shifter-fork shafts are tight in their bores, the gearbox front cover must be removed so that the

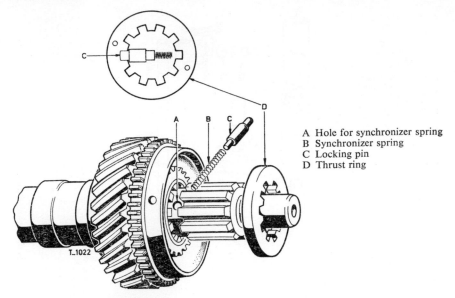

A Hole for synchronizer spring
B Synchronizer spring
C Locking pin
D Thrust ring

**Fig. 23. Synchromesh detail, location of spring-loaded plunger**

shafts can be driven out with a suitable soft drift.
(5) Remove the gearbox front cover; this is the cover which serves to retain the primary shaft ball-bearing and is secured by three nuts and lock washers; remove the cover with the gasket and the thrust washers. Do not remove the oil-seal from the cover, unless renewal is necessary.
(6) Remove the locating bolt and withdraw the reverse gear idler shaft, together with the gear.
(7) With the aid of a suitable drift, tap out the secondary shaft toward the front and carefully lower the cluster-gear assembly onto the bottom of the gearbox. Remove the mainshaft front ball-bearing housing and withdraw the mainshaft assembly from the gearbox.
(8) Remove the primary shaft, together with its ball-bearing, from the front of the gearbox; it may be necessary to assist removal by gently tapping with a drift. Temporarily reinstall the secondary shaft with the cluster-gear assembly, measure the cluster-gear end-float and make a note of the reading. Finally, remove the secondary shaft with the cluster gear and the thrust washers.

Do not dismantle the gearbox extension housing, unless the ball-bearing and/or the oil-seal need replacement. Removal of the oil-seal requires the use of tools 18G389 and 18G389C. After having removed the snap-ring, the rearmost ball-bearing can be removed from the housing. The new oil-seal should be installed with the aid of tool 18G134 and adaptor 18G134N.

*The primary shaft can be dismantled as follows:*
(9) Remove the bearing needles from the primary-shaft bore. Secure the primary shaft in a soft-jawed vice, bend back the locking plate and remove the bearing retaining nut with the aid of tool 18G5.

NOTE: *This nut has a left-hand thread.*

D

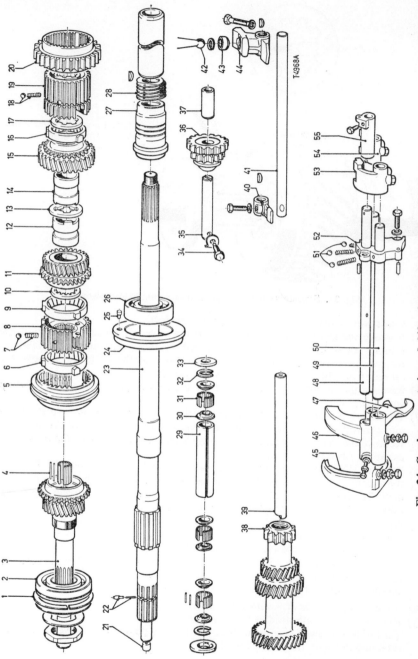

Fig. 24. Gearbox, gear trains and shifter fork mechanism, exploded view

(10) Press the ball-bearing from the primary shaft and remove the snap-ring from the bearing outer race.

(11) Dismantle the cluster-gear assembly as follows:
Remove the snap rings from both sides of the cluster gear and remove the bearing needles and the spacer bush.

(12) Before dismantling the mainshaft, measure the third-speed gear end-float, to ensure that upon assembly the correct thrust washer is used. Dismantle the mainshaft as follows: Remove the third/fourth gear front baulk ring, the synchro hub and sleeve, and the rear baulk ring. The synchro sleeve can be removed from its hub but take care to retain the detent balls and springs, which will be released.

(13) Depress the front thrust-washer retaining peg, rotate the thrust washer to align its internal splines with the splines on the mainshaft, and remove the washer.
Remove the third-speed gear with its bearing bush and remove the bush interlocking ring to free the second-speed gear. Remove the second-speed gear, the baulk-ring, bush and thrust washer, in that order.

(14) Remove the first- and second-speed synchromesh and gear. The first-speed gear may be removed from the hub, but care must be taken to retain the detent balls and springs, which will be released when the gear is withdrawn from the hub.

(15) Remove the speedometer drive gear with the Woodruff key and withdraw the distance piece from the shaft.

(16) Press the bearing from the shaft and remove the bearing from the gearbox housing.
Carefully clean and inspect all parts, replace all gaskets, lock washers and preferably the oil-seals. Examine the bearings for pitting and looseness, and renew if necessary.

*Key to Fig.* 24:

1 Bearing circlip
2 Ball-bearing
3 Main drive shaft
4 Needle roller bearing
5 Third/top-speed synchro sleeve
6 Synchronizer ring
7 Synchronizer spring and ball
8 Third/top-speed synchro hub
9 Synchronizer ring
10 Thrust washer
11 Third-speed pinion
12 Third-speed pinion bush
13 Interlocking ring
14 Second-speed pinion bush
15 Second-speed pinion
16 Second-speed synchronizer ring
17 Interlocking ring
18 Synchronizer spring and ball
19 Second-speed synchro hub
20 First-speed pinion
21 Spigot bearing oil resistor
22 Synchro hub locating peg assembly
23 Mainshaft
24 Bearing retainer
25 Locating peg
26 Ball-bearing
27 Distance sleeve
28 Speedometer drive gear
29 Spacer sleeve
30 Thrust washer for 31
31 Needle roller bearing
32 Circlip
33 Thrust washer
34 Reverse pinion shaft locating bolt
35 Reverse pinion shaft
36 Reverse pinion
37 Reverse pinion bush
38 Cluster gear
39 Secondary shaft
40 Selector lever, front
41 Remote-control shaft
42 Gearshift lever
43 Cup
44 Selector lever, rear
45 Third/top-speed shifter fork
46 First/second-speed shifter fork
47 Reverse speed shifter fork
48 Shifter-fork shaft for 46
49 Shifter-fork shaft for 45
50 Shifter-fork shaft for 47
51 Detent balls and springs
52 Shifter-fork shaft locating block
53 Reverse-speed selector dog
54 Third/top-speed selector dog
55 First/second-speed selector dog

*Assembling the gearbox:*

(1) Secure the secondary shaft in a vice; the recessed end of the shaft should be pointing downwards.

Liberally coat the shaft with grease and install the needle bearing, the spacer bush and the remaining two needle bearings on the shaft.

Fit a snap-ring into the front bore of the cluster gear and carefully lower it onto the shaft; take the assembly out of the vice and install the second snap-ring. Withdraw the shaft from the gear.

Place the cluster-gear assembly, together with the thrust washers, in the bottom of the gearbox. The thrust washers are available in four thicknesses to obtain correct end-float:      0·154–0·156 in
0·157–0·159 in
0·160–0·161 in
0·163–0·164 in

(2) Assemble the mainshaft as follows:

With the aid of tools 18 G 222 and 18 G 223, install the second-speed synchromesh hub and third and top-speed synchromesh hub, respectively.

(3) Press the rear ball-bearing into its housing and the bearing onto the shaft.

(4) Install the speedometer drive gear with the key, distance piece, lock washer and nut.

(5) Install the first-speed gear and second-speed synchromesh unit to the mainshaft, followed by the baulk-ring and the rear thrust washer.

(6) Install the second-speed gear bush, making sure that the lugs are turned towards the front and that the oil-hole in the bush corresponds with the oil-hole in the shaft.

(7) Install the second-speed gear and the interlock washer, so that the washer engages with the lugs on the bush.

(8) Press the third-gear bearing bush onto the shaft with the lugs facing the front. Ensure that the lugs engage the interlock washer and that the oil-hole and the cut-away in the bush line-up with the holes in the shaft.

(9) Install the retaining spring and peg, followed by the third-speed gear, with its cone face forward. Rotate the gear so that the hole in the cone lines up with the retaining peg: depress the peg with a thin drift, install the thrust washer and turn it so that it is locked by the peg.

Thrust washers are available in three thicknesses: 0·1565–0·1575 in
0·1585–0·1595 in
0·1605–0·1615 in

(10) Install the third-speed baulk-ring, the third/top-speed synchromesh unit, and the top-speed baulk-ring.

(11) Install the primary shaft assembly as a reversal of dismantling.

(12) Insert the assembled mainshaft from the rear of the gearbox; carefully enter the mainshaft spigot in the needle bearing of the primary shaft and push the mainshaft fully home.

(13) Carefully lift and align the cluster gear with the thrust washers and insert the secondary shaft; the cut-away end of the shaft should face forward.

(14) Install the reverse gear idler shaft with the gear and secure the shaft with the locating screw, using a new locking tab washer.

(15) Install the primary shaft bearing shims, align the cut-away of the secondary shaft with the inside edge of the gearbox front cover and install the front cover with a new gasket.

Assemble the clutch operating fork with the bolt and special nut.

(16) Install the shifter-fork shaft guide block to the rear face of the gearbox and insert the detent springs and balls.

(17) Fit the selector dogs to their respective shafts, securing them with the locating screws and locking wire.

(18) Depress the detent springs and insert the shifter-fork shafts, and install the reverse, first/second- and third/top-speed shifter-forks in that order. Do not forget to fit the spacer bush on the third/fourth-speed shaft and tighten the locknuts on each locating bolt.

(19) Install the gearbox side cover using a new gasket.

(20) Install the mainshaft distance piece onto the shaft; place a new extension housing gasket over the studs and install the extension housing.

Further assembly of the gearbox is a reversal of the dismantling procedure.

After installing the gearbox in the vehicle, install the remote control housing, using a new gasket, and fill the gearbox with the recommended lubricant.

For dimensions and tolerances refer to *Technical Data*.

**Overdrive:** The Laycock de Normanville overdrive unit, fitted as an optional extra, is electrically-operated from a facia-mounted switch.

This unit operates on top and third gear only.

The overdrive unit itself is fitted to the rear of the normal gearbox and takes the place of the normal rear extension housing.

*Operating principles:*

The overdrive unit incorporates an epicyclic gear train.

An epicyclic gear train consists of a sun gear, planet gears, a planet-gear carrier and an outer ring, the annulus.

If the planet carrier is rotated while the sun gear is locked to the annulus, the whole gear train will rotate as a solid unit, providing direct drive. If, on the other hand, the sun gear is locked to the casing, preventing it from rotating, and the planet carrier is rotated, the annulus will be driven at a higher speed than the planet carrier.

*Operation:*

In addition to an epicyclic gear train, there is a hydraulic pump, a roller clutch and a sliding cone clutch.

When in direct top gear the overdrive is inoperative. The drive from the gearbox to the propeller shaft would normally be transmitted by the rollers only from the gearbox mainshaft to the outer member of the uni-directional clutch, and so direct drive would be transmitted.

The roller clutch, however, drives in one direction only, and therefore, if the car were to over-run the engine, the rollers would be pushed down the inclined surfaces, away from the bore in the annulus or output member, and the drive would be broken, leaving the car without engine resistance to assist braking. This problem is overcome by means of a cone clutch. This cone clutch slides on the splined sun-gear extension and is spring-loaded to engage with the corresponding cone of the annulus, thus locking the sun gear to the annulus.

Between the annulus and the sun gear are the planet pinions, fitted to the planet carrier which is mounted on the driving shaft.

The planet pinions are therefore also locked and resistance to over-run is provided by the engine through the gearbox and mainshaft to the planet pinions.

When overdrive is engaged, a valve in the unit is opened, applying hydraulic pressure to two pistons, which work in cylinders formed in the unit housing. These pistons exert pressure against the cone clutch member, overcoming the

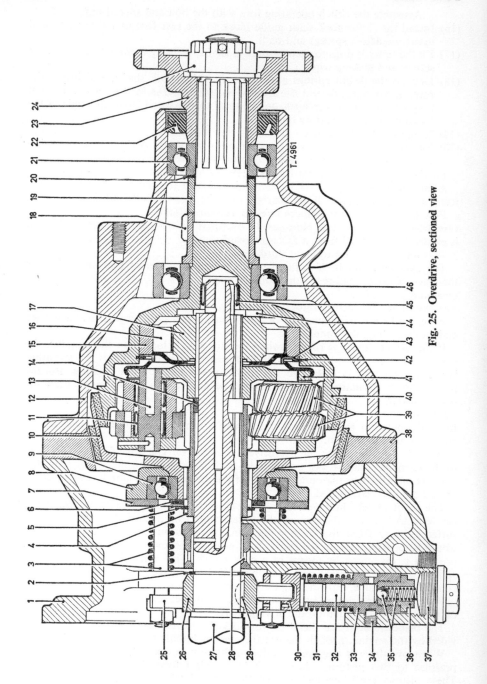

T-4961

Fig. 25. Overdrive, sectioned view

spring pressure and pushing the cone clutch away from the annulus until the outer lining presses against a conical brake ring built into the main housing.

The sun gear, which carries on its splined extension the cone clutch, is free to rotate on the driving shaft; therefore, when the cone clutch comes into contact with the brake ring, both cone clutch and sun gear are brought to rest and held stationary.

The planet carrier, which is splined to the driving shaft, is driven round the stationary sun wheel so that the planets rotate and drive the annulus at a higher speed than the driving shaft. In overdrive, the outer member of the roller clutch over-runs the inner member. Engine braking is again provided by the cone clutch, which prevents the sun gear from rotating in either direction.

*Construction:*

The gearbox mainshaft is extended to form the input shaft of the overdrive unit. This shaft carries a cam, operating a plunger-type hydraulic pump.

Further back on the shaft there is a freely rotatable sun gear in one piece with an externally splined sleeve. Immediately behind the sun gear and splined to the shaft, is the planet carrier in which are mounted the three planet pinions. At the rear of the input shaft and also splined to it is the inner member of the roller clutch. The outer member of the roller clutch is carried in the annulus, which is in one piece with the output shaft. Mounted on the splined sleeve of the sun gear is the one piece with the output shaft. Mounted on the splined sleeve of the sun gear is a double cone clutch member.

The cone clutch member can slide over the splined sleeve of the sun gear so that the inner lining can make contact with a corresponding cone in the annulus; alternatively, the outer lining can make contact with the cast-iron brake ring, which is mounted in the unit housing.

To the hub of the cone clutch member a ball-bearing is secured, housed in a flanged thrust ring. This ring carries on its forward face a number of pegs, acting as guides to compression springs, by which the cone clutch member is held against the annulus. The thrust ring has also four pins attached to it, which carry two

*Key to Fig. 25:*

| | | | |
|---|---|---|---|
| 1 | Overdrive housing | 24 | Retaining nut for 23 |
| 2 | Circlip | 25 | Bridge-piece |
| 3 | Clutch spring and special bolt | 26 | Eccentric cam |
| 4 | Sun gear | 27 | Input shaft |
| 5 | Circlip | 28 | Input shaft bearing bush |
| 6 | Thrust washer | 29 | Woodruff key |
| 7 | Ball-bearing retainer plate | 30 | Pump-plunger roller |
| 8 | Bearing retainer | 31 | Plunger spring |
| 9 | Ball-bearing | 32 | Pump plunger |
| 10 | Sliding clutch member | 33 | Plunger body |
| 11 | Needle roller | 34 | Locating screw |
| 12 | Overdrive housing, rear part | 35 | Check valve assembly |
| 13 | Planet-gear shaft | 36 | Check valve body |
| 14 | Circlip | 37 | Locating plug for 35 |
| 15 | | 38 | Brake ring |
| 16 | Uni-directional clutch | 39 | Planet gears |
| 17 | | 40 | Annulus |
| 18 | Speedometer drive gear | 41 | Planet carrier |
| 19 | Spacer bush | 42 | Circlip |
| 20 | Shim | 43 | Retaining ring |
| 21 | Ball-bearing | 44 | Thrust washer |
| 22 | Oil-seal | 45 | Needle roller |
| 23 | Propellor shaft coupling flange | 46 | Ball-bearing |

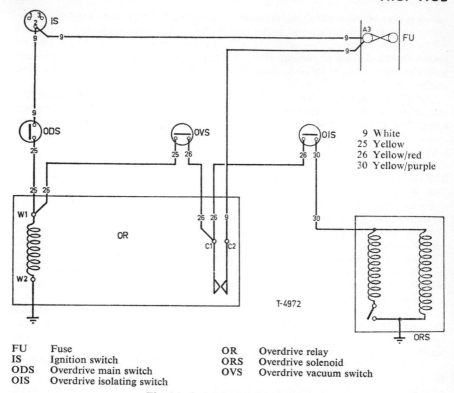

| FU | Fuse | OR | Overdrive relay |
| IS | Ignition switch | ORS | Overdrive solenoid |
| ODS | Overdrive main switch | OVS | Overdrive vacuum switch |
| OIS | Overdrive isolating switch | | |

Fig. 26. Overdrive, wiring diagram

bridge-pieces bearing against the pistons operating in cylinders formed in the unit housing.

The pistons can push in the opposite direction to the thrust of the springs and are connected through a valve to the overdrive oil pump.

In direct gear the drive from the input shaft is through the rollers of the roller clutch, which rise up the inclined faces of the inner member and become wedged between the inner and outer member of the roller clutch. The inner lining of the cone clutch is held locked by spring pressure against the annulus, so that the entire gear train rotates as a solid unit to prevent a freewheel condition and to handle reverse torque.

The change into overdrive is effected by operating a switch, which in turn actuates the solenoid. When the plunger is drawn into the solenoid, this rotates the operating shaft so that the cam lever lifts the operating valve spindle, admitting oil into the two cylinders in the unit casing, pushing the operating pistons against the bridge-pieces.

The cone clutch member now overcomes the clutch spring pressure and slides forward along the splines of the sun-gear extension, until the outer lining contacts the stationary brake ring.

The oil-immersed cone clutch comes smoothly to rest, together with the sun gear, resulting in a perfectly smooth change into overdrive. During the brief period of time when the change into overdrive is taking place, the power continues to be transmitted through the roller clutch until overdriving actually commences, so that the drive is without interruption and the change instantaneous. When changing from overdrive to direct drive, the throttle may be kept open. The release of oil pressure from the operating cylinders is deliberately restricted so that the cone clutch takes about half a second to move over to the direct drive position. As soon as contact between the cone clutch and the brake ring is broken, the load on the engine is released, allowing the engine to speed-up until the roller clutch ceases to be over-run and takes up the drive again. The change into normal drive is completed as the cone clutch contacts the annulus to prevent freewheeling.

*Electric control:*

The operating valve lever is lifted automatically by the plunger of an electric solenoid. The solenoid has two separate coil windings with an internal switch which is closed when the solenoid is not energised. The closing coil gives a powerful initial lift to open the valve, after which the internal switch opens, leaving the holding coil to continue holding the valve open.

*Dismantling:*

First remove the remote control mechanism by withdrawing its six attaching bolts and lock washers, as well as both screws of the rear support bracket.

The overdrive is mounted to the gearbox by means of an adaptor plate and is secured with eight studs. One of the attachment studs is longer than the others.

After evenly loosening the eight stud nuts, the overdrive unit can be removed.

Remove the control valve plug, thus allowing air to enter the overdrive pistons to facilitate their removal.

Remove the nuts securing the two bridge-pieces and remove them.

Withdraw the pistons with suitable pliers, giving a rotary pull.

After removal of the adaptor, the bolt securing the pump housing can be removed; then remove the non-return valve assembly and withdraw the pump housing.

The front and rear overdrive casings are held together by means of eight bolts and nuts; evenly slacken the nuts, thus slowly relieving the tension of the clutch springs. Remove the housing, together with the brake ring. Withdraw the four clutch springs from the special bolts on the pressure plate and remove the clutch mechanism, together with the sun gear.

The brake ring can be removed together with the housing; if necessary, the brake ring can be freed by gently tapping the flange with a copper mallet.

Remove the sun gear from the cone clutch after removing the snap ring from the front part of the sun-gear hub.

Next, remove the larger snap-ring and withdraw the thrust bearing from the housing as a unit.

Take the planet carrier from the annulus. If the uni-directional clutch is to be dismantled, the snap-ring and the brass ring, situated at the forward end of the clutch, should be removed.

Place tool 18G178 centrally over the clutch, which prevents the rollers from dropping out, and remove the inner part. Remove the thrust washer. The annulus is equipped with a caged needle bearing; removal of this bearing requires the use of a special extractor. After removing the speedometer drive gear and sleeve, which are located by a dowel, and withdrawing the coupling flange from the rear end of the unit, the annulus can be removed from the overdrive rear casing.

The front bearing can be removed together with the shaft, whereas the rear bearing remains in the casing.

Carefully clean and inspect all parts for wear or damage.

*Assembling the overdrive:*
Take care that all parts are meticulously cleaned before assembly, so that the operation of the hydraulic system is not adversely affected.

Install the annulus, the speedometer drive gear and the thrust washer between the front and rear ball-bearing into the overdrive rear casing. If a new bearing is fitted it is essential to re-determine the thickness of the aforementioned thrust washer as follows:

Place the annulus, together with the speedometer drive gear and the spacer, into the rear casing. With the aid of feeler gauges measure the distance between the rear ball-bearing abutment and the spacer. To this value add 0·005–0·010in, which gives the correct thickness of the thrust washer. The thrust washers are available in several thicknesses for selective fit to provide an output shaft end-float of 0·005–0·010in without pre-loading the bearings.

Install and secure the propeller-shaft coupling flange; observe the correct tightening torque of the nut. (*Technical Data.*)

Install the sleeve and speedometer drive gear, and locate with the dowel.

Assemble the uni-directional clutch. Make sure that the slots in the ratchet engage with the tongues on the roller cage and see that the spring rotates the cage so as to force the rollers up the ramps of the ratchet. The cage is spring-loaded anti-clockwise as seen from the front.

Place the assembly face downward into service tool 18G178 and install the rollers in the cage, whilst turning the freewheel clockwise.

Install the brass protector ring in front of the flywheel and secure it with the circlip.

In order to make sure that the double row of teeth of each planet gear meshes with the annulus teeth, each gear should be turned so that the scribed line is pointing radially outwards and corresponds with a similar scribed line on the carrier.

Temporarily install the sun gear; install the assembly to the annulus and remove the sun gear.

Note: As long as the planet carrier remains within the annulus, the sun gear can be removed or installed at any time; if, however, the carrier is taken out of the annulus, the lining-up procedure must be repeated.

Pass the sun-gear splines into the open end of the cone clutch and fit the snap-ring at the front end of the sun gear.

Press the thrust bearing into its housing, install the four thrust-ring bolts, and fit the complete assembly to the forward end of the cone clutch hub. Secure the assembly with the large snap-ring.

Fit the clutch mechanism onto the annulus, ensuring that the planet gears engage properly.

Install the pressure plate and the springs on the guide bolts. Fit the brake ring to the housing; the larger diameter of the tapered portion facing the rear of the housing (use a suitable jointing compound).

Carefully guide the shouldered bolts through the holes in the front housing; push the front half towards the rear in order to compress the clutch springs, and screw on the nuts. Make sure the shouldered bolts are not binding in their holes when gradually tightening the nuts until the two housing faces meet. Install the two operating pistons and carefully insert the rubber sealing rings into the cylinder bores (the centre spigot of the pistons must be towards the front). Install the two bridge-pieces and the lock washers, and tighten the nuts.

When the pump body has been removed, insert it with the small end in the centre plug opening of the overdrive housing. The oil inlet port in the annular groove in the pump body should be facing towards its port in the main housing.

Gently tap the pump body into position until the groove is in line with the lock bolt at the bottom of the housing. Tighten the lock bolt and install the pump valve, washer and plug. Screw in the relief valve assembly and plug in the right-hand side of the bottom. Support the unit in a vertical position and insert a dummy or a spare mainshaft into it, so that the splines of the planet carrier and those of the uni-directional clutch are brought into alignment; if necessary use a long, thin-bladed screwdriver to align the two parts prior to inserting the dummy shaft (turn anti-clockwise only). Ensure that the lower portion of the oil-pump drive cam contacts the pump plunger and that the retaining clip of the mainshaft is properly located in its groove.

Engage third or top gear and carefully guide the mainshaft into the centre sleeve. Slowly rotate the mainshaft back and forth to allow its splines to engage with those of the planet carrier. Before finally bolting the unit to the adaptor, make sure that the oil-pump plunger is properly seated on its operating cam. Finally, install the remote-control housing with a new gasket.

*Overdrive adjustment (unit installed in vehicle):*

The controls are correctly adjusted when a $\frac{3}{16}$ in diameter rod can be passed through the hole in the solenoid lever and into the hole in the overdrive housing. When performing this check, the ignition should be switched on, top gear engaged and the overdrive control switch in the overdrive position.

If the solenoid operates but does not move the setting lever far enough to allow insertion of the rod, the solenoid plunger has to be adjusted to prevent the closing coil being permanently energized (current draw 20A). Adjustment is as follows:

Push the plunger as far as possible into the solenoid and screw the self-locking nut in or out whilst the solenoid spindle is held with the aid of a suitable wrench.

When correctly set, the solenoid lever should just contact the nut when the $\frac{3}{16}$ in diameter rod is inserted. If the solenoid does not operate, check the electrical circuits according to the diagram (Fig. 26).

For additional dimensions and tolerances etc., refer to *Technical Data* on page 80.

**Propeller shaft:** The propeller shaft and the universal joints are of the Hardy Spicer type with needle bearings in the universal joints. The flanged rear end of the shaft carries the rear universal joint flange yoke, while the front end of the shaft is splined and engages a sleeve and yoke assembly. When assembled, the end of the sleeve and sliding yoke assembly are sealed with a dust cap, a steel and a cork washer.

The sliding yoke assembly is fitted with a grease nipple, while on early roadsters only each universal joint spider is also fitted with a grease nipple.

The propeller shaft flanges are secured to the gearbox drive flange and the rear axle companion flange respectively by means of four bolts, spring washers and Aerotight or Nyloc nuts.

NOTE: Prior to removing the propeller shaft, it is essential that both flanges are marked in relation to their mating flanges, so as to ensure correct replacement, thus maintaining the balance of the assembly.

**Rear axle/Differential:** Three-quarter floating rear axle with hypoid pinion and crownwheel. The differential assembly is mounted in a separate carrier, which can be removed from the axle housing without the necessity of removing the entire rear axle assembly from the car.

*Removal and installation of a drive shaft and brake drum:*

*Disc-type road wheels:*

Loosen the road wheel nuts, jack-up the car and remove the wheel.

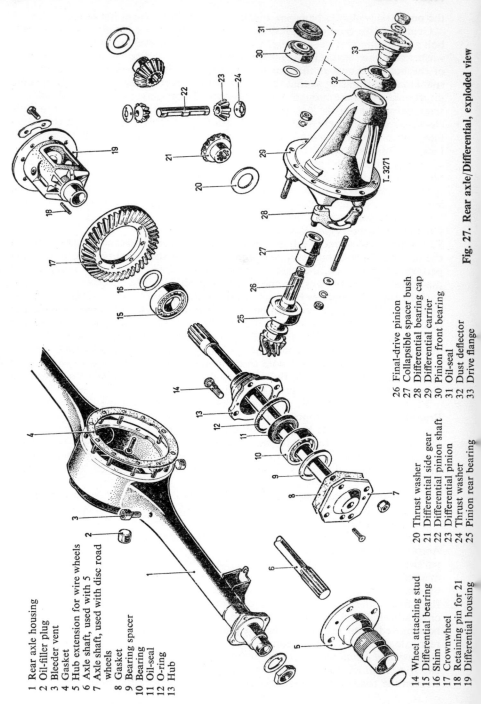

Fig. 27. Rear axle/Differential, exploded view

T.3271

1 Rear axle housing
2 Oil-filler plug
3 Bleeder vent
4 Gasket
5 Hub extension for wire wheels
6 Axle shaft, used with 5
7 Axle shaft, used with disc road wheels
8 Gasket
9 Bearing spacer
10 Bearing
11 Oil-seal
12 O-ring
13 Hub

14 Wheel attaching stud
15 Differential bearing
16 Shim
17 Crownwheel
18 Retaining pin for 21
19 Differential housing

20 Thrust washer
21 Differential side gear
22 Differential pinion shaft
23 Differential pinion
24 Thrust washer
25 Pinion rear bearing

26 Final-drive pinion
27 Collapsible spacer bush
28 Differential bearing cap
29 Differential carrier
30 Pinion front bearing
31 Oil-seal
32 Dust deflector
33 Drive flange

Remove the two countersunk brake drum retaining screws and tap the brake drum from the hub, using a soft-faced mallet. If difficulty is encountered in removing the brake drum, it may be necessary to back-off the brake shoe adjusters.

Remove the countersunk screw from the drive flange, after which the drive shaft can be removed by hand. It may be necessary to insert a thin-bladed screwdriver between the drive-shaft flange and the hub in order to obtain a better grip on the shaft.

Installation is a reversal of the removal procedure.

*Wire spoke type wheels:*

Remove the road wheel and remove the four nuts securing the brake drum to the hub; gently tap the brake drum from the hub. It may be necessary to back-off the brake shoe adjusters. Remove the countersunk screw from the drive-shaft extension; remove the extension and shaft. The extension flange has two tapped holes so that the shaft can be pulled out if it is tight.

Take care not to damage the sealing ring fitted between the hub and the extension.

Installation is a reversal of the removal procedure.

*Removal and installation of a hub:*

Remove the brake drum and drive shaft as outlined above and remove the bearing spacer. Bend back the tab of the locking washer and remove the nut with a suitable wrench.

Tilt the lock washer to dislodge the tab from the slot in the threaded portion of the axle casing and remove the locking washer.

Withdraw the hub, using a suitable extractor, such as service tools 18G304 and 18G304B.

The bearing and the oil-seal will be withdrawn together with the hub. The bearing is non-adjustable and is replaced in the conventional manner.

When reassembling, it is essential that the outer face of the bearing spacer protrudes by $0 \cdot 001$–$0 \cdot 004$ in beyond the outer face of the hub when the bearing is pressed into position; this ensures that the bearing is clamped between the abutment in the hub and the drive flange on the axle shaft.

*Removing and dismantling the differential unit:*

Drain the oil from the rear axle casing and remove both drive shafts as outlined on page 53 of this manual. Mark the position of the propeller shaft coupling flanges to ensure correct replacement, and disconnect the propeller shaft. Remove the 10 nuts securing the differential carrier to the rear axle casing; remove the differential carrier and the gasket. Mark the position of the differential bearing caps to ensure correct replacement and remove the bearing caps, followed by the differential unit. Drive out the differential pinion shaft locking pin; the diameter of this pin is $\frac{3}{16}$ in. In view of the taper bore in the differential housing, the locking pin should be driven out from the crownwheel side. It may be necessary to clear the bore in the housing in order to allow removal of the locking pin. Tap the differential pinion shaft out of the bore and remove the pinions, their thrust washers and the differential side gears.

Knock back the tabs of the locking plates and remove the crownwheel securing bolts from the differential housing; using a copper mallet, gently tap the crownwheel from the differential housing.

Knock back the tab of the locking plate and remove the pinion nut, the companion flange and the pressed end cover.

Tap the pinion rearward and out of the housing; it will carry with it the inner race and rollers of the rear bearing and the bearing spacer, leaving the front bearing assembly in position.

Remove the front bearing inner race by hand; the outer race of each bearing should be removed with tool 18G264 in conjunction with adaptors 18G264E and –F.

Slide off the pinion sleeve and adjustment shims; remove the rear bearing inner race with the aid of tool 18G47C and the adaptors 18G47AH.

Make a note of the thickness of the adjustment shim found behind the rear pinion bearing inner race.

Clean and inspect all parts; renew all gaskets and preferably the oil seals.

*Assembly and adjustment of the differential unit:*

Crownwheel and pinion are a matched set and can only be replaced as a mated pair. When fitting a new crownwheel and pinion the following operations must be carried out:

(a) Setting the pinion and crownwheel position; (b) adjusting the pinion bearing pre-load; and (c) adjusting the backlash between both the pinion and crownwheel.

Install the pinion bearing outer races; place a shim of known thickness behind the pinion head and press on the rear pinion bearing.

Install the pinion into the carrier (without shims, bearing spacer or oil-seal), install the pinion front bearing as well as the driving flange, and tighten the flange retaining nut until a pre-load of 10–12in lb is obtained.

Remove the keep disc from the base of the magnet and zero the dial indicator on the machined step 'B' on the gauge block of tool 18G191B. Position the magnet on the pinion head, with the foot of the dial indicator resting on the centre of the differential bore. Obtain the maximum depth reading and make a note of the difference from the zero position. Repeat this check in the opposite bearing bore and make a note of the mean reading.

The pinion is marked with a figure, etched in the pinion head, and will always be minus (—).

(a) If the gauge reading is minus, the gauge reading must be added to the pinion-head marking and the thickness of the shims be reduced by this value.

(b) If the gauge reading is plus, but numerically less than the pinion-head marking, the shim thickness must be reduced by the difference.

(c) If the gauge reading is plus, but numerically greater than the pinion-head marking, the shim thickness should be increased by the difference.

*Example (a):*

| | |
|---|---|
| Gauge reading: | —0·003 in |
| Pinion-head marking: | —0·002 in |
| Amount to be subtracted: | 0·005 in |

*Example (b):*

| | |
|---|---|
| Pinion-head marking: | —0·004 in |
| Gauge reading: | +0·003 in |
| Amount to be subtracted: | 0·001 in |

*Example (c):*

| | |
|---|---|
| Gauge reading: | +0·006 in |
| Pinion-head marking: | —0·003 in |
| Amount to be added: | 0·003 in |

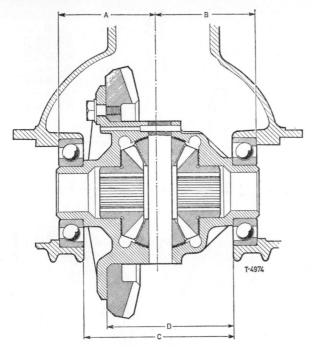

A Centre-line of differential unit to bearing shoulder in carrier on left-hand side.
B Centre-line of differential unit to bearing shoulder in carrier on right-hand side.
C Total distance between bearing shoulders of differential housing.
D Crownwheel mating face to bearing shoulder on right-hand side of differential housing.

T-4974

**Fig. 28. Rear axle/Differential, adjustment**

If the gauge reading is plus and numerically equal to the pinion-head marking, no correction is necessary. This also applies when an unmarked pinion is fitted and the gauge reading is zero.

The actual mounting distance (pinion depth adjustment) of the pinion is marked on the pinion head in a rectangular bracket. If the pinion marking is a plus figure, the shim thickness must be reduced by an equal amount. If the pinion marking is a minus figure, the shim thickness must be increased by an equal amount.

Remove the pinion, install the correct number of shims under the pinion head and assemble the bearings, the new spacer bush, the pre-load shims, a new oil-seal, and finally the driving flange. Tighten the flange retaining nut gradually to the torque figure of 140 ft lb. Make a frequent check of the pre-load, which should not be in excess of 13–15 in lb, or the spacer bush will be distorted and require replacement. If necessary, correction to the pre-load can be made by adding or removing shims between the spacer bush and the pinion front bearing. If the pre-load is too little, the shim thickness must be reduced; if too great, shims must be added. Determine the variation in differential bearing thickness:

Install a differential bearing on the small surface plate of tool 189191B, the inner race of the bearing over the recess and the side marked 'Thrust' facing downwards.

Place the magnetic gauge block onto the surface plate and zero the dial indicator on the machined step, marked 'B', of the smaller gauge block. Transfer the pointer to the plain surface of the bearing inner race and press the bearing firmly against the balls. Make a note of the reading thus obtained. A positive reading denotes the

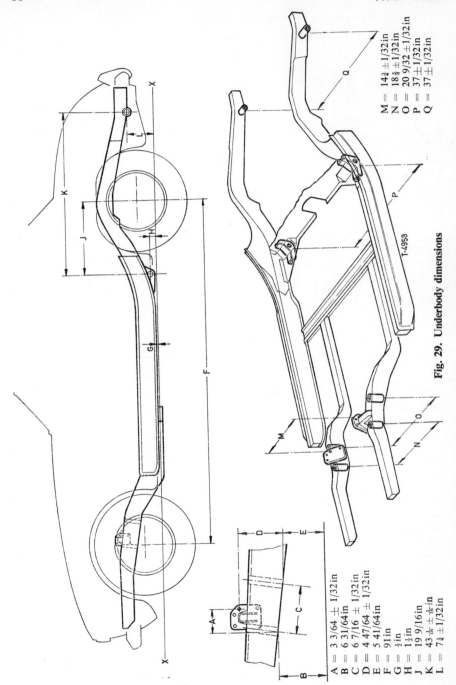

M = 14¾ ± 1/32in
N = 18⅝ ± 1/32in
O = 20 9/32 ± 1/32in
P = 37 ± 1/32in
Q = 37 ± 1/32in

T-4958

**Fig. 29. Underbody dimensions**

A = 3 3/64 ± 1/32in
B = 6 31/64in
C = 6 7/16 ± 1/32in
D = 4 47/64 ± 1/32in
E = 5 41/64in
F = 91in
G = ½in
H = 1¼in
J = 19 9/16in
K = 43 1/16 ± 1/16in
L = 7¼ ± 1/32in

thickness of the shimpack to be subtracted from the shims at this side; a negative reading indicates the thickness of the shimpack to be added (variations of standard width of bearings). Repeat this operation with the other bearing. Refer to Fig. 28. Variations of the dimensions A and B are stamped on the differential carrier, near the bearing bores, thus facilitating the calculation of the required shim thickness to obtain the necessary bearing pre-load. Variations of the dimensions C and D are stamped on the differential housing. The shimpack on the left-hand side is established as follows:

$$A+D—C+0\cdot007in$$

The shimpack on the right-hand side is calculated as follows:

$$B—D+0\cdot006in$$

The letters in the above formulae are to be substituted by the dimensional variations, stamped on the carrier and the housing.

Compose shimpacks as described and add the necessary corrections as outlined above. The back of the crownwheel is marked with a framed number; this must be taken into account before assembling the shims and bearings to the differential housing. If the framed number on the crownwheel is, e.g., minus one, a shim of $0\cdot001$in must be transferred from the right-hand side to the left-hand side (crownwheel side). If the number should be plus 2, a shimpack of $0\cdot002$in must be transferred from the left-hand side to the right-hand side. Press the differential bearings (thrust face outwards) and the shims onto the differential housing.

Assemble the differential side gears, the differential pinions, the thrust washers and the pinion shaft to the differential housing; insert the locking pin and peen over some of the surrounding material to lock the pin.

Attach the crownwheel to the differential housing and tighten the securing bolts to 60ft lb; at this stage do not bend over the tabs of the locking plates.

Place the assembly in 'V'-blocks and check the crownwheel run-out with the aid of a dial indicator. The maximum permissible run-out is $0\cdot002$in.

Only when the crownwheel is found to be true the tabs of the locking plates can be bent over.

Install the differential housing, together with the differential bearings, into the carrier; install the bearing caps in their original positions and tighten the bearing cap attaching nuts to 65ft lb.

Check the backlash with a dial indicator. The recommended backlash is etched on the crownwheel. Backlash should be within $0\cdot004$ and $0\cdot007$in. Backlash can be adjusted by moving the crownwheel in or out of mesh by transferring shims from one side to the other. Do not alter the total number of the shims.

The transfer of an $0\cdot002$in shim from one side to the other results in a variation in backlash of about $0\cdot002$in.

Further assembly of the differential is a direct reversal of the dismantling procedure.

Install the differential unit as a reversal of the removal procedure.

## CHASSIS

**Chassis:** Frame and body are welded together to form one rigid unit. See Fig. 29 for dimensions.

**Front suspension:** Independent front suspension by means of coil springs and wishbones of unequal length controlled by double-acting hydraulic shock-absorbers and (on some models) an anti-roll bar. The suspension units are mounted on a detachable front sub-frame which is secured to the body side-members by means of rubber mountings. This allows the entire front suspension to be removed as a

E

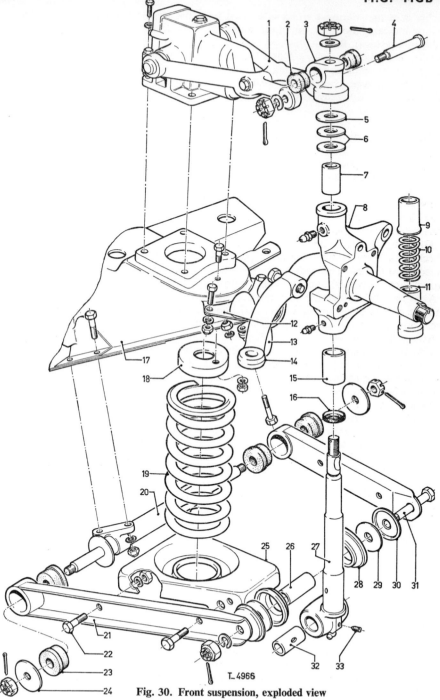

T. 4966

**Fig. 30. Front suspension, exploded view**

unit. The cross-member is fitted with two welded brackets providing a mounting for the steering rack.

The lower suspension arms are rubber-mounted on a pivot which is bolted to the sub-frame; the outer ends of the arms are bolted to the lower end of the wheel swivel. The upper suspension arms are formed by the piston-type shock-absorber arms; the shock-absorber is mounted on top of the sub-frame.

The outer end of the shock-absorber arms are secured to the swivel pin upper trunnion link by a fulcrum pin and tapered rubber bushes.

*Removal of the front suspension as a unit:*
Place the front of the car on suitable chassis stands and remove the front road wheels. Disconnect the anti-roll bar links (if fitted) from the spring pans.

Remove the steering rack as described on page 65 of this manual. Drain the hydraulic brake fluid and disconnect the brake pipes from the flexible hoses and from the retaining clips on the cross-member.

With the aid of a trolley-jack, support the cross-member at its centre point; remove the nuts and washers from the top of the support bolts, lower the assembly and remove it from under the car.

*Installation:*
Installation is a direct reversal of the removal procedure.

**Nylon-seated track-rod ball-joints:**
The ends of the track-rods are fitted to the steering arms by means of nylon-seated ball-joints, which were grease-packed in production and do not require periodic maintenance. As the entry of dirt or grit could easily ruin the nylon ball-joints, it is of utmost importance that the rubber dust boots are in good condition. If a dust boot is found to be torn or damaged, it is evident that foreign particles have already entered the ball-joint, in which case the entire ball-joint must be replaced. However, if the dust boot is accidentally damaged while servicing, it is safe to replace the dust boot only.

Before fitting a new dust boot, smear the adjacent area with some Dextragrease Super G.P.

On early models, a plain washer is fitted under the ball-joint securing nut.

Later models are fitted with steering arms which have a smaller diameter taper hole for ball-joint pin accommodation; the ball-joint pin on these models is longer and a heavier nut without washer is used.

When on earlier models (having a plain washer under the ball-joint securing nut), a new steering arm is fitted, the plain washer must not be replaced.

*Key to Fig.* 30:

| | | | |
|---|---|---|---|
| 1 | Shock-absorber | 17 | Chassis cross-member |
| 2 | Rubber bush | 18 | Coil spring locating plate |
| 3 | Upper trunnion | 19 | Coil spring |
| 4 | Fulcrum pin | 20 | Fulcrum shaft |
| 5 | Shim | 21 | Suspension arm |
| 6 | Thrust washers | 22 | Bolt |
| 7 | Swivel-pin upper bush | 23 | Rubber bushing |
| 8 | Front wheel swivel assembly | 24 | Plain washer |
| 9 | Dust excluder, upper | 25 | Spring seating plate |
| 10 | Spring | 26 | Spacer bushing |
| 11 | Dust excluder, lower | 27 | Swivel pin |
| 12 | Rebound rubber assembly | 28 | Dust excluder |
| 13 | Bump rubber | 29 | Thrust washer |
| 14 | Steering arm | 30 | Retainer for 28 |
| 15 | Swivel-pin lower bush | 31 | Outer fulcrum pin |
| 16 | Cork sealing ring | 32 | Lower fulcrum bush |
| | | 33 | Bush locating screw |

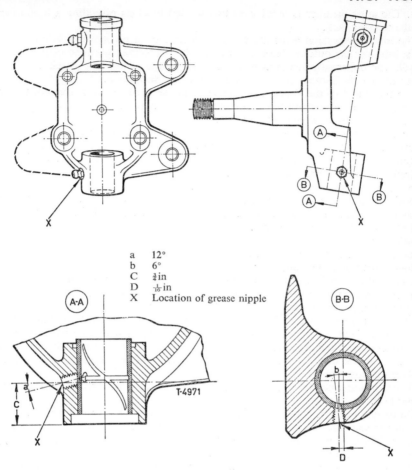

| | |
|---|---|
| a | 12° |
| b | 6° |
| C | ¾ in |
| D | ₁₆ in |
| X | Location of grease nipple |

T-4971

**Fig. 31. Front wheel swivel, grease nipple location (early type)**

*Front wheel hubs and bearings, removal and installation:*
Jack-up the front end of the car and remove the road wheel of the hub to be worked on.

Remove the two studs which secure the brake caliper to the swivel axle, and support the caliper clear of the swivel assembly.

Withdraw the hub cap, remove the split pin and unscrew the stub axle nut.

Withdraw the hub and brake disc assembly with the aid of a suitable extractor.

From the hub, remove the bearing retaining washer, the outer bearing, the adjustment shim(s), the spacer, the inner bearing, the oil-seal collar and the oil-seal, in that order. Unless replacement is necessary, the bearing outer races should be kept in the hub.

Carefully clean and inspect all parts, renewing those that are worn or damaged.

Wash out the bearings in paraffin and dry them with compressed air or with a non-fluffy rag. Examine the needle rollers for chips, pitting or other damage and for proper location in their cages. Carefully inspect the bearing inner and outer races for damage or wear.

Immerse the bearings in mineral oil to prepare them for assembly.

*Installation and bearing adjustment:*

Assemble the hub, omitting the adjustment shims at this stage, and install the assembly on the stub axle. Install the retaining washer and the nut; tighten the nut until the bearings just bind. Then remove the nut and washer and pull out the outer bearing race. Insert sufficient shims of known thickness to provide an excessive end-float. Refit the washer and the nut, and tighten the nut.

Accurately measure the bearing end-float, using a dial indicator. Remove the nut and washer, and remove as many shims as necessary to provide the required end-float. Shims are available in several thicknesses ranging from $0 \cdot 003$ in to $0 \cdot 010$ in.

Install the retaining washer and nut, and tighten the nut to a torque of between 40 and 70 lb ft. Install a new split pin and refit the hub cap.

Further assembly is a reversal of the removal procedure.

*Coil springs, removal and installation:*

Each coil spring is retained by a spring seat, bolted to the lower wishbone and a spigot bolted to the underside of the cross-member.

Compress the spring, using a suitable spring compressing tool, and remove the bolts securing the spring seat to the lower wishbones. Remove the anti-roll bar (if fitted). Slowly decompress the coil spring and remove it.

Installation is a direct reversal of the above operation.

*Front wheel swivels, removal and installation:*

Remove the road wheel and hub assembly as described on the previous page.

Remove the steering lever bolts and disconnect the lever.

Remove the disc cover plate after withdrawing its securing bolts. Remove the coil springs as outlined above.

Remove the split pins from the swivel fulcrum pin and trunnion pin, and remove the nuts.

Remove the centre-bolt and the clamp-bolt of the shock-absorber arm; ease the arm outward and remove the swivel with the stub-axle.

Dismantle the swivel assembly as follows:

Remove the split pin from the swivel axle and remove the nut, the upper trunnion suspension link, the steel and bronze thrust washers, the swivel pin, the dust caps and the spring, in that order. Remove the cork washer from the swivel pin.

If necessary the swivel-pin bushes can be replaced. After pressing in the new bushes (open end of oil groove first and lubrication hole in alignment with channel in axle), these should be line-bored to the finishing dimensions with the aid of a suitable set. For dimensions see *Technical Data.*

Examine the distance tube for wear; the correct length is $2 \cdot 337$ in. Check the thrust washers for scoring and wear; the thrust faces should be parallel within $0 \cdot 0005$ in; thickness should be $0 \cdot 065 – 0 \cdot 068$ in.

*Assembling and installation:*

Carry out the above in reverse order.

Check that the swivel-pin end-float is between $0 \cdot 008$ and $0 \cdot 013$ in.

**Front wheel alignment:** When checking the front wheel alignment, the car should be standing on absolutely level ground. The tyres should be inflated to the correct pressures. Bounce the car up and down several times so it will settle to the normal driving position and turn the front wheels to a dead straight-ahead position.

For specifications refer to *Technical Data.*

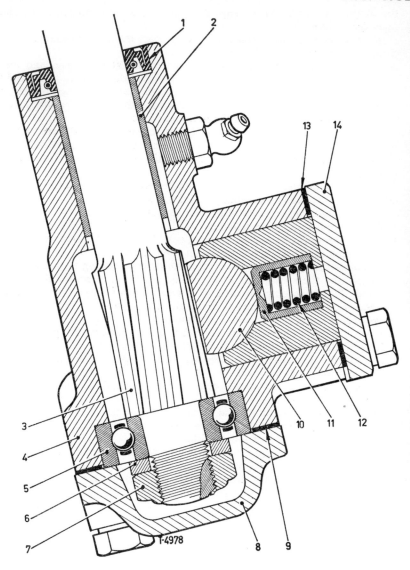

Fig. 32.  Steering gear, sectioned view

1 Oil-seal
2 Pinion shaft bush
3 Steering pinion
4 Steering housing
5 Ball-bearing
6 Spacer
7 Bearing retainer nut

8 Steering housing bottom cover
9 Gasket
10 Steering rack
11 Plunger
12 Spring
13 Gasket
14 Top cover plate

Caster and camber are accurately set during production and no adjustment should be necessary.

**Rear suspension:** Rear suspension by means of conventional semi-elliptical leaf springs and double-acting hydraulic shock-absorbers of the piston type.

The front eye and rear shackle of each spring are fitted with rubber bushes. When fitting rear springs, do not tighten the spring eye-bolts or shackle nuts until the normal load is applied to the spring, so that the flexible rubber bushes are deflected to an equal extent in both directions during service. Neglect of these precautions will inevitably lead to early deterioration of the rubber bushes.

**Shock-absorbers:** Hydraulic shock-absorbers of the piston type. The dampers are set during production and no attempt should be made to dismantle them without the use of special tools. Shock-absorbers which do not function properly should be replaced. From time to time the fluid level in the reservoirs should be checked; for topping-up the rear shock-absorbers, access holes are provided, covered by rubber plugs, in the rear floor panel next to the battery cover.

**Steering gear:** The steering gear is of the direct-acting rack-and-pinion type; it consists of a rack bar and toothed pinion and is mounted on the front suspension cross-member.

The steering inner column is coupled to the pinion by means of a universal joint.

*Removal from the car:*

Support the front end of the car by placing chassis stands beneath the lower suspension arm spring seats and remove both front wheels.

Remove the locknuts and disconnect the track-rods from the steering arms. Turn the steering to the left lock (or right lock on left-hand drive cars) and remove the pinch-bolts of the universal joint at the pinion shaft. Remove the bolts and nuts securing the rack housing to the cross-member, observing the shims which may be installed between the rack and the frame brackets.

Finally, remove the steering assembly from underneath the car.

*Installation:*

Installation is a reversal of the removal procedure; however, be sure to place the steering wheel as well as the front wheels in a dead straight-ahead position when connecting the related parts.

*Dismantling:*

Secure the rack housing in a soft-jawed vice; remove the pinion end-cover and its gasket. Position a container to collect the oil that will drain from the housing.

Remove the damper cover and shims; next remove the yoke, the damper pad and the damper spring. Withdraw the pinion, together with the ball-race and the locknut, taking care not to damage the upper oil-seal. Bend back the lock washer and unscrew the ball-joint assemblies. Remove the dust boot clips and the boots. Prise up the indentations in the locking rings clear of the slots in the rack and ball housing. Slacken-off the locking ring and unscrew the housing, thus releasing the tie-rod, the ball seat and the seat tension spring.

Withdraw the rack bar from the pinion end of the housing.

**Note: Do not remove the rack from the other end or damage to the rack housing bush will occur.**

To remove the rack-housing bush, remove the self-tapping screw retaining it and carefully drive the bush out.

*Assembling and adjusting:*

Insert the rack-housing bush and carefully drive or press it in until it is flush with the housing end. Enter a 7/64 in diameter drill through the retaining screw hole and drill the bush to take the self-tapping locating screw.

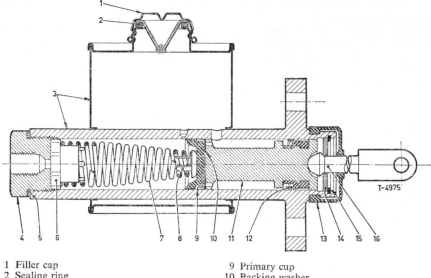

**1** Filler cap
**2** Sealing ring
**3** Master cylinder body
**4** Adaptor plug
**5** Sealing ring
**6** Check-valve assembly
**7** Piston return spring
**8** Spring guide

**9** Primary cup
**10** Backing washer
**11** Piston
**12** Secondary cup
**13** Dust boot
**14** Push-rod abutment washer
**15** Circlip
**16** Push-rod

**Fig. 33. Brake master cylinder**

In order to obtain a perfect oil tightness, smear the head of the screw with jointing compound prior to installation.

Insert the rack bar from the pinion end; install the ball seat spring, the ball seat, the tie-rod and the ball-housings, liberally smearing the ball seats with SAE 90 EP oil. Tighten the ball housings until the tie-rod is held firm and without free-play.

When correctly adjusted, a torque of 32 to 52 lb in should be necessary to articulate the tie-rods. Lock the housing by tightening the locking ring to a torque of 33–37 lb ft; secure the ring by punching the tabs of the locking ring into the slots in the ball-housing and rack. It is recommended that new locking rings are fitted whenever these have been disturbed.

Insert the pinion, with ball-race and locknut, into its housing.

Install the pinion end-cover and seal; use jointing compound to obtain an oil-tight seal. The outer edge of the ball race locking nut should then be peened over into the slot in the pinion shaft.

Adjust the rack damper assembly as follows:

Install the plunger and tighten down the cover without the spring or shims, until it is just possible to rotate the pinion shaft by sliding the rack bar through its housing.

With the aid of a feeler gauge, measure the gap between the cover and the housing; to this value add 0·003 to 0·005 in, which gives the correct thickness of shims to be placed beneath the damper retaining plate.

Remove the retaining plate and plunger and replace the assembly, using sealing compound to obtain an oil-tight seal.

Install the rubber boots with the retaining clips. Stand the rack housing on end and pour in one third of a pint of SAE 90 EP oil through one end of a dust boot, or pump it into the housing through the nipple provided.

**Brakes:** Hydraulically-operated foot brake on all four wheels, employing Lockheed self-adjusting disc brakes at the front and conventional, manually-adjustable drum-type brakes at the rear.

The brake master cylinder with integral brake fluid reservoir is mounted on the engine side of the bulkhead, just above the brake pedal. The fluid level in the reservoir should never be higher than ¼ in below the bottom of the filler neck and never be lower than half-full.

**Brake master cylinder:**

*Removal and installation:*
Withdraw the brake and clutch master cylinder cover retaining screws and remove the cover.

Drain the brake fluid by attaching a small-diameter rubber hose to a brake caliper bleed screw; open the bleed screw one full turn and depress the brake pedal. Hold the pedal depressed and close the bleed nipple; then let the pedal return to its normal position. Repeat this procedure until all fluid has thus been expelled from the system.

Remove the split pin, the washer and the pivot pin from the operating push-rod and disengage the brake pedal lever.

Disconnect the hydraulic pipeline and cap the cylinder union to prevent ingress of dirt.

Remove the assembly from the bulkhead after withdrawing the securing bolts.

*Dismantling and reassembling:*
Remove the rubber dust boot and slide it along the push-rod.

Depress the push-rod to relieve the load on the circlip. Remove the circlip and withdraw the push-rod assembly.

From the cylinder bore remove the piston, the piston washer, the primary cup, the spring retainer and check valve assembly—in that order.

Remove the secondary cup by easing it over the end of the piston.

Carefully clean all parts in clean brake fluid or methylated spirit. It is of paramount importance that scrupulous cleanliness is observed when handling parts of the brake master cylinder. Before installing the parts into the cylinder bore, be sure that the compensating port in the cylinder is clear.

Replace any parts that are worn or damaged, or whose serviceability seems doubtful.

Dip all parts in brake fluid of the recommended type and install them into the cylinder bore in reverse order of dismantling.

The brake master cylinder free-play is non-adjustable; if the unit does not function satisfactorily, the trouble is due to defective parts within the cylinder.

**Front disc brakes:** The front disc brake units are of the rotating disc and rigidly mounted caliper type; each caliper carries two operating pistons and two friction-pad assemblies, between which the brake disc revolves.

*Renewing the disc brake friction pads:*
Apply the parking brake, jack-up the front of the car and remove the road wheel. Depress the friction pad retaining springs, remove the split pins and retaining springs, and withdraw the friction pads.

When the friction lining has worn down to the minimum permissible thickness of $\frac{1}{16}$ in, the friction pads must be replaced. Before new friction pads can be inserted,

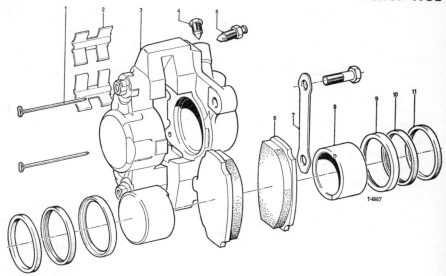

1 Brake pad retaining pin
2 Brake pad retainer
3 Caliper assembly
4 Plug
5 Bleeder screw
6 Brake pedal

7 Locking plate for caliper mounting
8 Piston
9 Dust seal retainer
10 Dust seal
11 Inner seal

**Fig. 34. Disc brake, exploded view**

the operating pistons, which will be at their maximum adjustment, must be returned to the base of their cylinder bores with the aid of a suitable clamping device. If necessary the bleed nipples can be opened to facilitate this operation; however, in that case, the system should be bled afterwards.

**Note: If the bleed nipples are not opened, upon forcing back the caliper pistons, the fluid level in the brake fluid container may rise excessively and thus overflow. To prevent this, siphon off any surplus fluid beforehand.**

Insert the new friction pads and ensure that these can move freely. Operate the brake pedal several times to take up any play and top-up the brake fluid level.

If necessary, bleed the brakes.

*Dismantling and reassembling the caliper:*

Remove the two bolts securing the caliper to the swivel assembly and withdraw the caliper. Do not disconnect the hydraulic hose, and support the caliper to avoid stretching the hose.

Remove the friction pads and clean the exterior of the caliper to prevent entry of dirt.

Hold the piston in the mounting half of the caliper with a suitable clamp and gently apply the footbrake until the free piston protrudes so far from its bore that it can be removed by hand. Have a clean receptacle handy to collect the spilt fluid. With a blunt tool remove the seal from the groove in the cylinder bore, taking great care not to damage bore or seal.

Remove the seal dust retainer by inserting a screwdriver between the retainer and the seal; gently prise the retainer from the mouth of the caliper bore. Then remove the rubber seal. In order to remove the piston from the mounting half of

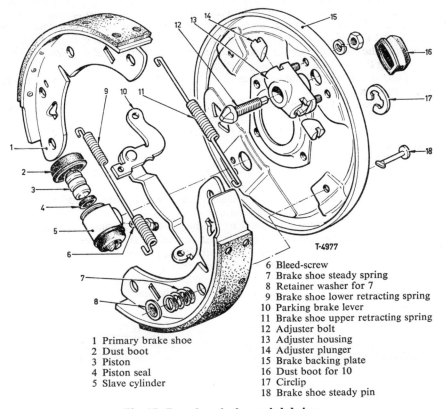

T-4977

6 Bleed-screw
7 Brake shoe steady spring
8 Retainer washer for 7
9 Brake shoe lower retracting spring
10 Parking brake lever
11 Brake shoe upper retracting spring
12 Adjuster bolt
1 Primary brake shoe          13 Adjuster housing
2 Dust boot                   14 Adjuster plunger
3 Piston                      15 Brake backing plate
4 Piston seal                 16 Dust boot for 10
5 Slave cylinder              17 Circlip
                              18 Brake shoe steady pin

Fig. 35. Rear drum brake, exploded view

the caliper it is necessary first to install the rim-half piston and then proceed as outlined above.

Thoroughly clean the caliper with the recommended brake fluid or methylated spirit. Other cleaning agents may damage or dissolve the internal rubber seal between the two caliper halves. Reassembly is an actual reversal of the dismantling procedure. Take great care not to tilt the pistons when pressing them into the caliper bores.

Note: **Unless absolutely unavoidable, do not separate the two caliper halves.**

If separation is unavoidable, the fluid channel seal, the clamping bolts and the locking plates must be replaced. On assembly the clamping bolts must be tightened to a torque of between 35·5 and 37 lb ft.

**Rear drum brakes:**
The rear brakes are of the leading and trailing shoe type; the parking brake mechanically operates each brake shoe by means of linked levers.

*Dismantling:*
Jack-up the car and remove the road wheel. Remove the brake drum as outlined on page 55 and fully slacken-off the brake adjuster.

Remove the brake shoe centralizing washer, spring and pin from each brake shoe. Pull one brake shoe radially outwards against the return spring action and disengage the shoe from its anchor points; the second brake shoe can then be removed by unhooking its return springs. Remove the wheel cylinder by disconnecting the hydraulic supply pipe at the rear of the brake backing plate, and withdrawing the circlip and retaining washer.

Disconnect the parking brake cable at the operating lever by removing the split pin and the pivot pin.

If necessary, the adjustment plungers can be withdrawn and the adjustment housing removed from the backing plate.

From the wheel cylinder remove both dust boots, the pistons, the cups and the spring.

*Reassembling:*

Reassembling is a reversal of the above operations. In addition, however, the following points should be observed:

Carefully clean all parts, particularly the internal wheel cylinder parts, and scrupulously examine their condition.

The wheel cylinder parts should be cleaned with the recommended brake fluid, after which they should be installed in wet condition. A serviceable wheel cylinder should have a smooth bore, free from scratches, pits or grooves. When doubting serviceability, do not hesitate to install new parts.

The brake shoes are interchangeable; when replacing, the brake shoe return springs should be on the backing plate side of the shoes and hooked-in as shown in Fig. 35.

*Rear brake adjustment:*

Excessive brake pedal free travel generally indicates that rear brake shoe adjustment is necessary; to this end, jack-up the rear of the car and fully release the parking brake. Turn the square-headed adjusting bolt projecting from the upper part of the brake backing plate in a clockwise direction until the wheel is blocked; then turn back one notch only. The wheel should now be freely rotatable without the brake linings dragging. Adjust the other rear wheel brake in a similar manner.

*Parking brake adjustment:*

Adustment of the brake shoes, as outlined above, automatically adjusts the parking brake; if, however, the parking brake lever free travel remains excessive, the length of the operating cable should be reduced by turning the brass adjusting nut at the lower end of the parking brake lever, below the car floor.

Correct adjustment is obtained if the parking brake is applied fully when the lever is pulled up three or four notches.

## BODY

*Door lock and window winding mechanism:*

In order to gain access to either mechanism, proceed as follows:

Remove the centre screw of the inner door handle and the window operating crank; withdraw the handle and the crank, the escutcheons and the fibre washers. Remove the door pull and the locking knob (on the passenger door). Remove the screws securing the trim panel to the door, and remove the waist rail securing screws at its ends. After the trim panel is removed, the remaining waist rail attachment screw will be exposed and can be removed if necessary.

Remove the inside trim liner which is glued to the door panel.

*Window winding mechanism, removal and installation:*

Release the rear window guide upper and lower mountings, wind the glass to the uppermost position and release the regulator arm and idler arm brackets; slide both arms toward the front and out of the window bottom guide rail. Carefully lift the glass from the door. Remove the four screws securing the regulator arm brackets to the door panel and withdraw the mechanism through the rear access hole in the door panel.

Installation is a direct reversal of the removal procedure; note that most of the mechanism securing holes are elongated to allow some degree of adjustment.

*Door locks, removal and installation:*
Detach the remote-control link by unscrewing the two screws, and remove the three remote-control mechanism attaching screws. Remove this mechanism through the rear access hole in the door panel. Remove the two outer door handle securing screws and disengage the handle from the lock. Working from the inside of the door panel, remove the circlip from the door lock barrel and withdraw the barrel with the coupling link from the door.

Remove the four door lock securing screws and withdraw the lock.

Installation is a reversal of the removal operations.

Correct adjustment of the remote-control mechanism is possible by elongated securing holes. After installation, lubricate and check for proper functioning.

*Instruments:*
The instruments are each secured by means of a bridge-piece and two knurled nuts.

For removal proceed as follows: Disconnect the battery and detach the connections from the unit in question. Withdraw the illumination and warning lamp bulb sockets and remove the knurled securing nuts with the bridge-piece. Remove the gauge with its rubber packing from the instrument panel. The combined water temperature/oil pressure gauge, as well as the fuel gauge, are removed in a similar manner; however, when removing the combined gauge, the water temperature bulb must be detached from the engine.

Installation is a reversal of the removal instructions.

*Windscreen-wiper motor, gearbox and wheelboxes—removal and installation:*
The wiper motor and gearbox are situated beneath the facia on the passenger's side and are secured to the bulkhead by three screws.

Remove the wiper arms, the electrical connections at the motor and disconnect the outer cable at the gearbox housing. Remove the three screws securing the mounting bracket to the bulkhead panel and remove the assembly. Slacken the cover screws of each wheelbox and remove the cable rack outer casings.

The wheelboxes can be withdrawn after removal of the nut, the front bush and sealing washer on the scuttle.

Installation is a reversal of the above procedure.

## ELECTRICAL EQUIPMENT

**Electrical system:** 12-volt, positive (+) terminal connected to earth. The two 6-volt series-connected batteries are located just forward of the rear axle, in separate containers. Access to the batteries is gained after removing the moulded carpet and the battery compartment cover. For specifications refer to *Technical Data* in the back of this manual.

**Generator:**
*Dismantling:*
Remove the drive pulley securing nut and withdraw the pulley and the Woodruff key from the armature shaft. Remove the two through-bolts and remove the commutator-end cover. Withdraw the pulley-end cover, together with the armature and its ball-bearing, from the yoke.

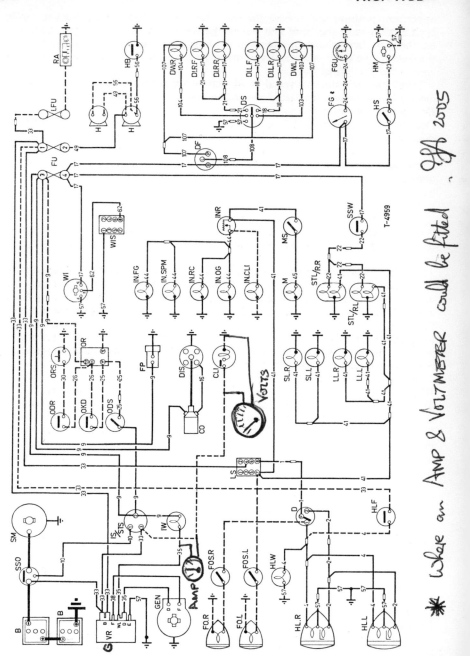

**Fig. 36. Wiring diagram, early models**

Unless the ball-bearing is worn or damaged, its removal from the cover is unnecessary; if required, the bearing must be pressed out by means of a suitable handpress after the retaining plate rivets have been drilled out. Thoroughly clean all parts and carry out the following inspection:

Check the condition of the carbon brushes and ensure that these can move freely in their holders; if this is not the case, they should be polished with a smooth file.

If the brushes are worn or broken, new brushes must be fitted and properly bedded on the commutator. This can be performed by wrapping a strip of very fine sandpaper around the commutator and pressing the brushes in their holders against the commutator, which should then be turned by hand until the brushes are seated properly on the commutator. The commutator should be smooth and free from pits, burrs or burnt-in spots. Clean the commutator with a soft cloth soaked in petrol and if necessary polish it with a strip of very fine sandpaper.

A badly worn commutator should be skimmed in a lathe turning at high speed and employing a sharp tool; undercut the insulation to a depth of 1/32 in, after which the final polishing should be done with very fine sandpaper. (See *Technical Data*).

*Key to wiring diagrams (Figs. 36 and 37):*

| | | | |
|---|---|---|---|
| B | Battery | HLW | Main beam warning light |
| CLI | Cigar lighter | HM | Heater motor |
| CO | Coil | HS | Heater motor switch |
| D | Dimmer switch | IN | Instrument light |
| DF | Direction-indicator flasher | INR | Instrument light rheostat |
| DI.L.F | Direction-indicator, left front | IS/STS | Ignition/starter switch |
| DI.R.F | Direction indicator, right front | IW | Ignition/generator warning light |
| DI.R.R | Direction-indicator, right rear | LFU | Line fuse |
| DI.L.R | Direction-indicator, left rear | LL | Number-plate lamp |
| DIS | Distributor | LS | Light switch |
| DS | Direction-indicator switch | M | Map light |
| DW.L | Direction-indicator warning light, left | MS | Map light switch |
| | | ODR | Overdrive governor switch |
| DW.R | Direction-indicator warning light, right | ODS | Overdrive main switch |
| | | OG | Oil pressure gauge |
| FG | Fuel gauge | OKD | Overdrive kick-down switch |
| FGU | Fuel tank gauge unit | OR | Overdrive relay |
| FO.R | Fog lamp, right | ORS | Overdrive solenoid |
| FO.L | Fog lamp, left | RA | Radio |
| FOS | Fog lamp switch | RC | Revolution counter |
| FP | Fuel pump | SL.L | Sidelamp, left |
| FU | Fuses in fuse-holder | SL.R | Sidelamp, right |
| GEN | Generator | SM | Starter motor |
| GVR | Gauge voltage regulator | SPM | Speedometer |
| H | Horn | SSO | Starter solenoid |
| HB | Horn button | STL/R.R | Stop lamp/rear lamp, right |
| HL.L | Headlamp, left | STL/R.L | Stop lamp/rear lamp, left |
| HL.R | Headlamp, right | WI | Windscreen-wiper |
| HLF | Headlamp flasher contact | WIS | Windscreen-wiper switch |

*Colour code to wiring diagrams (Figs. 36 and 37):*

| | | | | | | | |
|---|---|---|---|---|---|---|---|
| 1 | Blue | 21 | Green/white | 33 | Brown | 56 | Purple/black |
| 2 | Blue/red | 22 | Green/purple | 35 | Brown/yellow | 57 | Black |
| 4 | Blue/white | 23 | Green/brown | 38 | Brown/green | 62 | Black/white |
| 9 | White | 24 | Green/black | 41 | Red | 103 | Light green/yellow |
| 10 | White/red | 25 | Yellow | 44 | Red/white | 104 | Light green/blue |
| 16 | White/black | 26 | Yellow/red | 45 | Red/green | 106 | Light green/green |
| 17 | Green | 30 | Yellow/purple | 49 | Purple | 107 | Light green/purple |
| 18 | Green/red | | | | | 108 | Light green/brown |

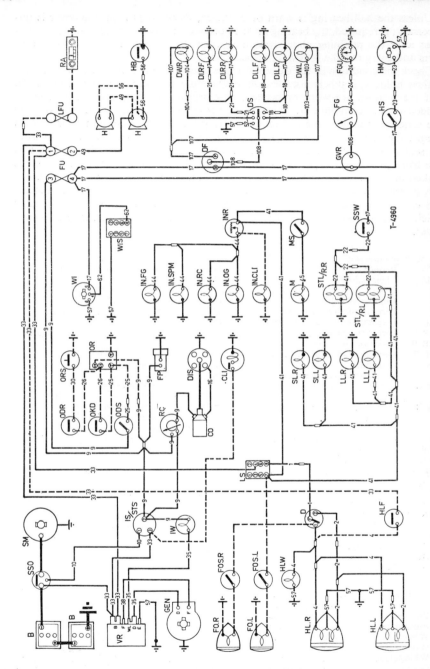

**Fig. 37. Wiring diagram, later models**

The field coils may be tested *in situ* by means of an Ohm-meter (the reading should be 6·0–6·3 Ohms), or by connecting a 12-volt battery with an ammeter in series between the field coil terminal and the yoke. The ammeter reading should be approximately 2 Amps. No reading indicates an open circuit, necessitating renewal of the coils.

An ammeter reading considerably more than 2 Amps or an Ohm-meter reading of much less than 6 Ohms is evidence of a short circuit in one of the field coils. Install new field coils as necessary.

The armature should be checked with a growler and voltage drop-test equipment; if these are not available, check the armature by substitution. The bearing bush can be removed by means of a suitable extractor or by screwing a ⅝ in tap into it, after which it can be withdrawn.

NOTE: Before pressing in a new porous bronze bearing bush, it should be immersed in light engine oil for 24 hours (or for two hours in oil heated to 100°C). Do not ream the bush or the porosity will be impaired.

When pressing the pulley-end cover onto the armature shaft, be sure to support the inner bearing race *and not the end cover;* this operation is best accomplished with a piece of tube.

*Reassembly:*

After thorough examination of all parts, renewing those that are worn or damaged, reassembly is effected in reverse order of the dismantling procedure, paying particular attention to the following:

If the ball-bearing is to be renewed, the new bearing should be packed with high-melting point grease before pressing it into the end cover, preceded by the oil-seal retaining washer, the felt washer and the corrugated washer. After the bearing has been pressed home, the bearing retaining plate must be secured with new rivets.

When installing the commutator-end cover, complete with the brush gear, the brushes must be held clear of the commutator by partially withdrawing them from their holders until the brush springs push them sideways against the holders, thus keeping them in this lifted position. Once the end cover is on the shaft and the distance between the cover and the yoke amounts to approximately ½ in, the brushes should be released onto the commutator with a small hook or screwdriver. Before finally pressing-on the end cover, ensure that the brush springs are properly seated on the brushes.

**Starter motor:**

NOTE: Before dismantling, note that the commutator and the brush gear can be examined without dismantling the starter motor. In order to check the brush gear, it is sufficient to remove the starter motor cover band. If the brushes are sticky and cannot move freely in their holders, they should be pulled out and lightly dressed with a smooth file. If the commutator is blackened or dirty, it can be cleaned by holding a soft cloth soaked in petrol against it whilst rotating the armature by hand.

*Dismantling:*

Lift the brush springs and pull the brushes clear of their holders.

Remove the terminal nuts and washer from the terminal post on the commutator-end cover.

Remove the two through-bolts and remove the commutator-end cover.

Remove the drive-end cover, together with the armature and drive assembly.

*Examining and reconditioning:*

The correct brush spring tension of 25–15 oz should be checked with a spring-

F

balance; if necessary, replace the springs. Chipped, cracked, worn or otherwise impaired brushes should be replaced by unsoldering the flexible connections and soldering the new brush connection to the terminals. Replacement brushes are pre-formed, which makes bedding on the commutator unnecessary.

The commutator must be smooth and free of pitted or burnt spots. Clean the commutator with a soft, petrol-moistened cloth; if this gives unsatisfactory results, carefully polish the commutator with very fine sandpaper. A badly damaged commutator must be skimmed in a high-speed lathe, using a sharp tool. Do not remove more material than is necessary.

**Note: Do not undercut the insulation between the segments.**

The field coils can be tested by connecting a 12-volt lamp with a 12-volt battery to the tapping point of the coils to which the brushes are soldered and the field terminal post.

If the lamp does not light up, there is an open circuit in the field coils, in which case they should be renewed. If the lamp does light up this does not necessarily mean that the field coils are in good order, as a short-circuited coil will also cause the lamp to light. This condition may be checked by removing the test lead from the brush connector and connecting it to the yoke instead; if the lamp lights up now, it is certain that the coils are short-circuited.

The armature core may under no circumstances be machined, nor should it be attempted to true a distorted armature shaft.

If the porous armature bearing bushes are worn to such an extent that renewal is imperative, follow the procedure as outlined under **Generator.**

The drive assembly can be withdrawn from the shaft after the spring has been compressed and the circlip has been removed.

Carefully clean and examine all parts and renew them as necessary.

*Reassembly:*

Reassembly is a reversal of the dismantling procedure.

# Technical Data

**Engine** (see also page 13):

| | |
|---|---|
| Engine type: | 18G, 18GA, 18GB |
| Bore: | 3·16in (80·26mm) |
| Stroke: | 3·5in (88·9mm) |
| Cubic capacity: | 109·6cu in (1798cc) |
| Capacity of combustion chambers (valves fitted): | 2·59–2·65cu in |
| Cylinder bore, first oversize: | 0·010in |
| maximum oversize: | 0·040in |

**Valves:**

| | |
|---|---|
| Valve head diameter, inlet: | 1·562–1·567in |
| exhaust: | 1·343–1·348in |
| Valve stem diameter, inlet: | 0·3422–0·3427in |
| exhaust: | 0·3417–0·3422in |
| Valve stem to valve guide clearance, inlet: | 0·0015–0·0025in |
| exhaust: | 0·002–0·003in |
| Valve face angle, inlet and exhaust: | 45° 30' |
| Valve lift, inlet and exhaust: | 0·3645in |

| Valve springs: | *outer* | *inner* |
|---|---|---|
| Length uncompressed: | 2 9/64 in | 1 31/32 in |
| Length, installed: | 1 9/16 in | 1 7/16 in |
| Spring tension, installed: | 72 lb | 28–32 lb |
| Spring tension, valve opened: | 117 lb | 48–52 lb |
| Valve bounce speed, engine rpm: | 6200 | |

**Valve guides:**

| | |
|---|---|
| Length, inlet: | $1\frac{5}{8}$ in |
|        exhaust: | 2 13/64 in |
| Outer diameter, inlet and exhaust: | 0·5635–0·5640 in |
| Bore diameter, inlet and exhaust: | 0·3442–0·3447 in |
| Interference fit in cylinder head: | 0·0005–0·00175 in |
| Height above cylinder head: | $\frac{5}{8}$ in (fitted) |

**Valve tappets:**

| | |
|---|---|
| Type: | barrel-type |
| Outer diameter: | 13/16 in |
| Length: | 2·293–2·303 in |

**Valve timing:**

| | |
|---|---|
| Valve rocker clearance (for checking valve timing only), inlet and exhaust: | 0·021 in |
| Inlet opens: | 16° B.T.D.C. |
| Inlet closes: | 56° A.B.D.C. |
| Exhaust opens: | 51° B.B.D.C. |
| Exhaust closes: | 21° A.T.D.C. |

**Valve rockers and valve rocker shaft:**

| | |
|---|---|
| Valve running clearance, engine cold: | 0·015 in |
| Valve rocker bore diameter: | 0·7485–0·7495 in |
| Rocker bush bore diameter: | 0·6255–0·6260 in |
| Valve rocker ratio: | 1·4 : 1 |
| Valve rocker shaft length: | 14 1/32 in |
| Valve rocker shaft diameter: | 0·624–0·625 in |

**Pistons:**

| | |
|---|---|
| Type: | solid-skirt type |
| Piston clearance, top of skirt: | 0·0036–0·0045 in |
|        bottom of skirt: | 0·0018–0·0024 in |
| Number of piston rings: | 4 (3 compression rings, one oil-control ring) |
| Width of piston ring grooves, | |
|        top ring: | 0·064–0·065 in |
|        second ring: | 0·064–0·065 in |
|        third ring: | 0·064–0·065 in |
|        oil control ring: | 0·1578–0·1588 in |
| Piston pin bore: | 0·7501–0·7503 in |
| Piston pin bore, 18GB engine: | 0·8126–0·8129 in |

**Piston rings:**

*Compression rings:*

| | |
|---|---|
| Top ring type: | chrome-hardened, parallel |
| Second and third compression rings: | cast-iron, taper |
| Width (all three rings): | 0·0615–0·0625 in |
| Ring gap (all three rings): | 0·012–0·017 in |
| Clearance in groove (all three rings): | 0·0015–0·035 in |

*Oil control ring:*

| | |
|---|---|
| Type: | slotted control ring |
| Width: | 0·1552–0·1562in |
| Ring gap, fitted: | 0·012–0·017in |
| Clearance in groove: | 0·0016–0·0036in |

**Piston pins:**

| | 18G/18GA engine | 18GB engine |
|---|---|---|
| Type: | semi-floating | fully-floating |
| Outer diameter: | 0·7499–0·7501 | |
| Fit in position: | hand-push fit | |

**Connecting rods:**

| | |
|---|---|
| Type: | angled big-end |
| Length between centres: | 6·5in |

**Big-end bearings:**

| | |
|---|---|
| Material: | steel-backed, copper/lead-plated |
| Width: | 0·995–1·005in |
| Radial clearance: | 0·001–0·0027in |
| Bearing end-float, nominal: | 0·008–0·012in |
| Available undersizes: | 0·010, 0·020, 0·030, 0·040in |

**Main bearings:**

| | |
|---|---|
| Number, 18G/18GA engine: | 3 |
| 18GB engine: | 5 |
| Bearing width, 18G/18GA, all bearings: | 1⅛in |
| Bearing width, 18GB engine, 1st, 3rd and 5th: | 1⅛in |
| 2nd and 4th: | ⅞in |
| Bearing clearance: | 0·001–0·0027in |
| Available undersizes: | 0·010, 0·020, 0·030, 0·040in |

**Crankshaft:**

| | |
|---|---|
| Main bearing journal diameter: | 2·1265–2·1270in |
| Crankpin diameter: | 1·8759–1·8764in |
| Crankshaft end-float taken at: | centre main bearing |
| Crankshaft end-float: | 0·002–0·003in |

**Camshaft:**

| | |
|---|---|
| Bearing journal diameter, front: | 1·78875–1·78925in |
| centre: | 1·72875–1·72925in |
| rear: | 1·62275–1·62325in |
| Bearing bush inside diameter, front: | 1·79025–1·79075in |
| centre: | 1·73025–1·73075in |
| rear: | 1·62425–1·62475in |
| Bearing clearance: | 0·001–0·002in |
| Camshaft end-float: | 0·003–0·007in |
| Cam lobe lift: | 0·250in |
| Timing chain, pitch: | ⅜in |
| number of pitches: | 52 |

**Oil pump:**

| | |
|---|---|
| Make and type: | Hobourn-Eaton concentric rotor-type |
| Pump capacity: | 3¼ Imp gall/minute at 2000 rpm |

Relief valve spring,
|  |  |  |
| --- | --- | --- |
| | free length: | 3 in |
| | fitted length: | 2 5/32 in |
| | tension when fitted: | 15·5–16·5 lb |
| Relief valve opens at: | | 70 lb/sq in |
| Oil pressure, normal engine speed: | | between 50 and 80 lb/sq in |
| | idling speed: | between 10 and 25 lb/sq in |

**Carburettors:**
| | |
| --- | --- |
| Make and model: | SU, HS.4 (twin) |
| Throat bore: | 1½ in |
| Jet size: | 0·090 in |
| Jet needles, standard: | No. 5 |
| rich: | No. 6 |
| lean: | No. 21 |
| Colour of piston damper spring: | red |
| Air-cleaners, make and type: | Cooper; replaceable paper element |

**Fuel pump:**
*Early models:*
| | |
| --- | --- |
| Make, type and model: | SU electrical, model HP |
| Minimum pump capacity: | 7 Imp gall/hour |
| Pump pressure (pumping height): | 4 ft |
| Minimum starting voltage: | 9·5 volts |

*Later models:*
| | |
| --- | --- |
| Make, type, and model: | SU electric, model AUF 300 |
| Minimum pump capacity: | 15 Imp gall/hour |
| Suction capacity (depth): | 18 in |

**Ignition system:**
*Coil:*
| | |
| --- | --- |
| Make and model: | Lucas HA12 (oil-filled) |
| Resistance primary coil at 68°F: | 3·1–3·5 Ohms (cold) |
| Current draw (ignition switched on): | 3·9 Amps |
| at 2000 rpm: | 1·4 Amps |

**Ignition distributor:**
| | |
| --- | --- |
| Make and model: | Lucas, 25D4 |
| Dwell angle: | 60° ±3° |
| Opening angle: | 30° ±3° |
| Automatic advance: | centrifugal and vacuum |
| Contact points gap: | 0·014–0·016 in |
| Contact points spring tension: | 18–24 oz |
| Condenser capacity: | 0·18–0·24 microfarads |
| Timing marks: | pointer on timing cover and notch on crankshaft pulley |

Static ignition setting,
| | |
| --- | --- |
| high compression: | 10° B.T.D.C. Octane rating 98/100 |
| low compression: | 8° B.T.D.C. Octane rating 95/97 |
| Radio suppressors (in high-tension leads): | Lucas W55; type L.2 |
| Automatic advance starts at: | 200 rpm |
| Maximum advance, high compression: | 20° at 2200 rpm (crankshaft degrees) |
| low compression: | 24° at 4400 rpm (crankshaft degrees) |

Vacuum advance,
    at 13 in Hg, high compression:     20° (crankshaft degrees)
    at 12 in Hg, low compression:      16° (crankshaft degrees)
*Advance test data at decreasing engine speed (in crankshaft degrees):*
*high compression ratio*                     *low compression ratio*
20° at 2200 rpm                              24° at 4400 rpm
15° at 1600 rpm                              18° at 3000 rpm
 9° at  900 rpm                               9° at 1000 rpm
 6° at  700 rpm                               8° at  800 rpm
 3° at  600 rpm                               3° at  600 rpm

**Spark plugs:**
Make and type:                      Champion N–9Y
Size:                               14 mm by ¾ in
Electrode gap:                      0·024–0·026 in

**Cooling system:**
Type:                               pressurised, with water pump, fan and
                                      thermostat
Thermostat setting, standard:       82°C (180°F)
                  hot climates:     74°C (165°F)
                  cold climates:    88°C (190°F)
Radiator filler cap relief valve
            opens at:               7 lb/sq in
Number of fan blades:               three, angled at 24°
Fan belt, width:                    ⅜ in
          length, outside:          35·5 in
          thickness:                5/16 in
          tension:                  ½ in on longest run
Water-pump type:                    impellor, belt-driven

**Clutch:**
Make and type:                      Borg & Beck, single dry plate,
                                      hydraulically actuated diaphragm-type
Clutch disc diameter:               8 in
Colour of diaphragm spring:         dark blue
Friction material:                  Mintex H.22 woven yarn
Number of damper springs:           six
Clutch throw-out bearing:           graphite (MY3D)
Clutch fluid:                       Lockheed disc brake fluid (Series II)

**Gearbox and overdrive:**
Speedometer gear ratio, standard:   9/28
                  with overdrive:   5/12
Synchronizer springs:
          free length:              ½ in
          fitted length:            5/16 in
          tension when fitted:      4–5 lb
Mainshaft end-float:                0·004–0·006 in
Cluster gear end-float:             0·002–0·003 in
*Overdrive:*
Make:                               Laycock de Normanville
Pump spring, free length:           2·00 in
                  rate:             11 lb in

| | |
|---|---|
| Clutch spring, free length: | 1·510in |
| rate: | 154lb in |

**Propellor shaft:**

| | |
|---|---|
| Type: | open tubular shaft with sliding yoke |
| Universal joints: | Hardy Spicer with needle roller bearings |
| Angular movement: | 18°–20° |
| Total length, fully extended (std): | 30¾in |
| overdrive: | 31⅞in |
| fully compressed (std): | 29 1/16 in |
| overdrive: | 30 3/16 in |
| Length of propellor shaft, standard: | 25 11/32in |
| overdrive: | 26 15/32in |
| Shaft diameter: | 2·00in |

**Rear axle/differential:**

| | |
|---|---|
| Type: | Hypoid, threequarters floating |
| Ratio: | 3·909 : 1 |
| Differential bearing pre-load: | 0·002in each |
| Pinion bearing pre-load: | 7–9lb in |
| Distance of spring axis: | 37·0in |

**Steering gear:**

| | |
|---|---|
| Type: | rack-and-pinion |
| Steering wheel diameter: | 16½in |
| Number of turns, lock to lock: | 2·93 |
| Turning circle: | 32ft |
| Universal joint: | Hardy Spicer KO518, GB166 |
| Pinion end-float: | 0·002–0·005in |
| Steering damper end-float: | 0·0005–0·003in |
| Toe-in: | 1/16 –3/32in (unladen) |
| Steering lock angle of outer wheel, inner wheel turned 20°: | 18° |

**Front suspension:**

| | |
|---|---|
| Type: | independent, with wishbones and coil springs |
| Spring diameter (mean): | 3·238in |
| free length: | 9·9±1/16 in |
| length at load of 1030lb: | 7±1/32in |
| maximum deflection: | 4·34in |
| Spring rate: | 348lb in |
| Camber angle: | 1° |
| Caster: | 7° }unladen |
| King pin inclination (KPI): | 8° |
| Shock-absorbers: | Armstrong, lever-type |
| Front wheel bearing end-float: | 0·002–0·004in |

**Rear suspension:**

| | |
|---|---|
| Type: | semi-elliptical leaf springs |
| Number of spring leaves: | six (seven on GT) |
| Spring leaf width: | 1¾in |
| Total length (fitted): | 44in |
| Free camber, measured alongside leaf: | 4·04in |
| Spring rate: | 93lb in |
| Shock-absorbers: | Armstrong, lever-type |

**Brakes:**
Type:                                    Lockheed hydraulic, disc type front
                                                                 drum type rear

Brake fluid:                             Lockheed disc brake fluid (Series II)
*Front brakes:*
Brake disc diameter:                     $10\frac{3}{4}$ in
Brake pad friction material:             DON55
Brake lining area:                       203 sq in
*Rear brakes:*
Brake drum diameter:                     10 in
Friction material:                       DON 24
Effective friction area:                 $106 \cdot 8$ sq in
Brake lining area:                       9 7/16 x $1\frac{3}{4}$ x $\frac{3}{16}$ in
**Electrical equipment:**
Batteries:                               6 volts SG9E or STGZ9E (twin)
Earthing:                                positive
Battery capacity:                        51 Ah at 10-hour rate
                                         58 Ah at 20-hour rate

**Control box:**
Make, model and type:                    Lucas RB340, 3-coil type
Operating voltage at 3000 rpm:
               at 10°C (50°F):           $14 \cdot 7$–$15 \cdot 7$ volts
                   20°C (68°F):          $14 \cdot 5$–$15 \cdot 5$ volts
                   30°C (86°F):          $14 \cdot 3$–$15 \cdot 3$ volts
                   40°C (104°F):         $14 \cdot 1$–$15 \cdot 1$ volts
Current setting at 4000 rpm:             22 Amps
Cut-out relay, cut-in voltage:           $12 \cdot 7$–$13 \cdot 3$ volts
                 cut-out voltage:        $9 \cdot 5$–11 volts
**Generator:**
Make, model and type:                    Lucas C 40/1, 12 volts, two-brush type
Cut-in speed:                            1585 rpm at $13 \cdot 5$ volts
Field coil resistance:                   $6 \cdot 0$ Ohms at 20°C (68°F)
Brush spring tension:                    22–25 oz
Minimum permissible brush length:        $\frac{9}{32}$ ins.
**Starter motor:**
Make, model and type:                    Lucas M418G, 4-brush type
Lock torque:                             17 lb ft at 340 Amps
Torque at 1000 rpm:                      8 lb ft at 250–270 Amps
Brush spring tension:                    32–40 oz
Starter drive ratio:                     $13 \cdot 3$ : 1
Minimum permissible brush length:        5/16 in
**Windscreen-wiper motor:**
Make, model and type:                    Lucas Dr. 3A, single-speed
Drive:                                   cable rack and wheelboxes
Armature end-float:                      $0 \cdot 008$–$0 \cdot 012$ in
Current consumption (running):           $2 \cdot 7$–$3 \cdot 4$ Amps
Number of strokes:                       45–50 per minute
Wiping angle:                            106° (earlier models 150°)
**Horns:**
Make, model:                             Lucas 9H, 12 volts
Maximum current draw:                    $3 \cdot 5$ Amps

# GENERAL FAULT FINDING CHART
# FOR PETROL ENGINES

Some items in this chart are not applicable to *every* make of petrol engine.

## Engine will not start

| | |
|---|---|
| **A. Starter does not crank engine** | |
| Battery run down | *Recharge; replace if defective* |
| Battery posts and terminals loose or corroded | *Clean and tighten. If badly corroded, soak with water to facilitate removal and avoid damage to the battery posts* |
| Faulty starter switch or solenoid, if fitted; broken battery cable or loose connection | *Check wires and cables; check solenoid and switch, replace if defective* |
| Starter motor defective | *Repair or replace* |
| Starter drive stuck (starter will run, but does not crank engine) | *Clean and if necessary repair or replace* |
| Starter drive pinion jammed with starter ring gear | *Free by rotating squared end of starter spindle with a spanner* |
| **B. Starter cranks engine slowly** | |
| Battery partly run down | *Recharge; replace if defective* |
| Loose or corroded connections | *Clean and tighten* |
| Faulty starter switch or solenoid; partly broken cable or loose connection | *Check wires and cables; check solenoid and switch, replace if necessary* |
| Starter motor defective | *Repair or replace* |
| **C. Starter cranks engine, but engine will not start** | |
| *Trouble in ignition system:* | |
| *No spark at plugs:* | |
| Moisture on spark plugs, ignition distributor, coil and wires (this trouble often occurs after parking overnight in foggy or rainy weather) | *Clean and dry. Avoid recurrence by coating wires, distributor rotor, cap, coil and spark plug insulators with moisture-proof lacquer* |
| Spark plugs flooded, due to excessive use of choke | *Start engine on full throttle. If this does not help, clean plugs. With plugs removed, turn over the crankshaft a few times to blow the accumulated fuel from the cylinders* |

| | |
|---|---|
| Spark plugs oiled-up | *Clean; if necessary replace* |
| Spark plug insulator cracked | *Replace* |
| Spark plug gap too wide or too close | *Reset gap* |
| *No spark at distributor:* | |
| Loose, broken or shorted low-tension lead between coil and/or inside distributor | *Check and tighten; also check internal leads in distributor. These leads sometimes break inside their insulation, and the break is not always visible. Pull carefully on one end; a broken lead will stretch* |
| Cracked rotor or distributor cap | *Replace* |
| Contact breaker points dirty, worn or maladjusted | *Clean and adjust; if necessary replace* |
| Carbon brush in distributor cap not making contact | *Free; if necessary replace* |
| Faulty condenser | *Replace* |
| *No spark at coil:* | |
| High-tension lead loose or broken | *Replace* |
| Broken or loose low-tension leads or faulty ignition switch | *Check wiring, repair or replace; check switch, replace if defective* |

| | |
|---|---|
| **D. Starter cranks engine, but engine will not start** | |
| *Trouble in fuel system:* | |
| *No petrol in carburettor:* Empty fuel tank | *Fill up. If necessary, check and repair or replace fuel gauge* |
| Obstructed or damaged fuel pipe Air leak in petrol line | *Clean; if necessary repair or replace* *Check and repair or replace. Pay special attention to flexible fuel line (if fitted). If flexible fuel line is porous, a temporary 'get-you-home' repair can often be made by securely wrapping the line with friction tape or rubbing with hard soap* |
| Fuel filter clogged | *Clean and refit with new gasket. Always carry a spare gasket and a glass filter bowl, if so equipped* |

| | |
|---|---|
| Fuel pump defective | *Repair or replace. If electric pump does not function, lightly tap pump housing until ticking resumes* |
| *Petrol in carburettor:* | |
| Jets clogged | *Clean; blow out with air (never use wire to clean jets)* |
| Float needle stuck | *Clean or replace* |
| Carburettor flooded | *Clean float needle valve; if necessary replace. If this trouble persists, check fuel pump pressure* |
| Choke control faulty | *Repair or replace* |
| Air leak at inlet manifold or carburettor base | *Check nuts and bolts for tightness; if necessary replace gaskets* |
| Water or dirt in carburettor | *Clean. If this trouble persists, check rubber hose in fuel tank filler neck for damage or looseness, causing water to enter tank* |

NOTE : *If ignition system and carburettor are in order, yet the engine will not start, check timing.*

## Engine starts but does not run properly

**E. Engine misfires**

| | |
|---|---|
| *Ignition trouble:* | |
| Spark plug or coil leads loose or damaged | *Tighten; replace if necessary* |
| Incorrect spark plug gap | *Regap* |
| Cracked spark plug insulator | *Replace faulty spark plug* |
| Spark plug oiled-up | *Clean, if necessary replace with spark plug of correct type. If trouble persists, check for mechanical trouble* |
| Cracked distributor cap | *Replace* |
| Loose connection in primary circuit | *Check and repair. Also check, and if necessary replace, ignition switch. In rare cases the ammeter has been found to be the cause of this trouble, due to faulty internal connection* |
| Distributor otherwise faulty | *See* **C** |
| *Trouble in fuel system:* | *See* **D** |

*Mechanical trouble:*

| | |
|---|---|
| Incorrect valve clearance | *Adjust* |
| Valve sticking | *Try to free by pouring a gum solvent of good quality into carburettor air intake; if not successful, dismantle and repair* |
| Valve spring broken | *Replace. Usually the valve concerned will have to be ground* |
| Worn piston, piston rings and cylinder or burnt valve; cylinder-head gasket blown | *Test compression; if too low, dismantle for repairs* |

**F.  Engine starts and stops**

| | |
|---|---|
| *Trouble in ignition or fuel system:* | *See* **C** *and* **D** |
| Obstructed exhaust system | *Check and repair or replace* |

**G.  Engine runs on wide throttle only**

| | |
|---|---|
| Idle jet clogged or mixture improperly adjusted | *Clean idle jet and/or idle air bleed; adjust* |
| Valve sticking or burnt; valve spring broken; other mechanical trouble | *Check and repair. Pay special attention to heat riser, if so equipped, since a burnt heat riser will cause exhaust gas to enter intake manifold. This will sometimes cause backfiring in carburettor* |

**H. Lack of power**

| | |
|---|---|
| Ignition too far retarded or other ignition trouble | *Check and correct (see* **C**) |
| Obstructed exhaust system | *Dented exhaust pipe and/or muffler Dislocated baffle plate in muffler Replace* |
| Trouble in fuel system | *Check and correct (see* **D**) |
| Loss of compression | *Test compression; if found to be too low, check valve clearance. If valve clearance is properly adjusted and compression is still low, check for other mechanical trouble, such as burnt valves and/or worn pistons, rings and cylinders* |
| Dragging brakes | *Check and correct. Essentially this is not an engine trouble* |

**I. Engine runs roughly**

| | |
|---|---|
| Ignition timing incorrect | *Check and correct. Pay attention to possibly stuck advance mechanism, because the fixed advance may be correctly adjusted, yet the timing while running will be incorrect if the automatic advance is stuck* |
| Lean or rich mixture | *Check carburettor and fuel system, (see* **D***)* |
| Improperly adjusted valve clearance | *Check and correct* |

**J. Engine knocks**

| | |
|---|---|
| Ignition too far advanced | *Check and correct. Attend to possibly stuck advance mechanism (see* **I***)* |
| Excessive carbon deposit | *Decarbonize* |
| Loose bearings or pistons or other mechanical cause | *Check and repair* |

**K. Engine overheats**

*Cooling system:*

| | |
|---|---|
| Lack of water | *Top-up and check for leaks* |
| Fan belt loose or broken | *Check and adjust or replace* |
| Radiator clogged by insects | *Clean* |
| Cooling system clogged internally (in water-cooled engines) | *Clean with a cooling system cleaner of a reputable make and flush out according to maker's instructions. Inspect radiator hoses and replace if in bad condition* |
| Thermostat stuck or faulty | *Check and replace if necessary* |
| Ignition improperly timed | *Check and correct. Attend to possibly stuck advance mechanism* |
| Lean or rich mixture | *Check fuel system (see* **D***)* |
| Excessive carbon deposit | *Decarbonize* |
| Obstructed exhaust system | *Check and repair or replace* |
| Cylinder-head gasket of the incorrect type | *Replace* |